JOSEPH SHUMAN
JOURNALISM COLLECTION

POINT PARK COLLEGE

THE A. S. W. ROSENBACH FELLOWSHIP
IN BIBLIOGRAPHY

JOURNALS and JOURNEYMEN

JOURNALS
and
JOURNEYMEN

A Contribution to the
History of Early American Newspapers

by CLARENCE S. BRIGHAM
Rosenbach Fellowship in Bibliography

GREENWOOD PRESS, PUBLISHERS
WESTPORT, CONNECTICUT

Contents

Illustrations

Introduction

◆◆

The present lectures are an outgrowth of my *Bibliography of American Newspapers,* constituting chapters on certain aspects of early newspaper history. Begun in 1913 and tentatively completed in 1927 (having been printed in eighteen installments in the *Proceedings* of the American Antiquarian Society) the compiling of the *Bibliography* required travel of about ten thousand miles and examination of files in nearly four hundred towns and cities in thirty different states, including all those east of the Mississippi River and also Arkansas, Louisiana, and Missouri.

Although I read only a small proportion of the many files, as a historian of journalism would have done, hundreds of interesting features connected with newspaper history were noted. With such a vast field to cover, and working entirely alone, the task could never have been finished if I had let myself into the pleasant byway of reading the papers. Yet unconsciously much information was absorbed and many facts remembered. Lately I grouped these facts by subject, and they form the basis of the present contribution to the Rosenbach Fellowship. At one time I had thought somewhat of prefacing the *Bibli-*

ography with a history of newspapers, at least for the period previous to 1820. But Frank Luther Mott's splendid and comprehensive *American Journalism,* published in 1941, made such an introduction unnecessary. Nor in fact had I prepared the *Bibliography* with such a history in view. Therefore the Introduction was a summary, statistical largely, of the ground covered, a listing of leading files and holdings, and a history of the development of the collections in the important newspaper-collecting libraries.

When I tried to decide upon a title for these lectures, I thought of several, such as "Memoranda regarding Early American Newspapers," "Sidelights on Early Newspaper History," or "Stray Notes for a History of Journalism." One discerning critic, thinking that the title ought to center around the word "Bibliography," humorously suggested that it be called "Ravelings from my Bib." At any rate the title finally used—"Journals and Journeymen—A Contribution to the History of Early American Newspapers"—will have to do.

When I wrote my Introduction I featured the statement that it was my old friend Professor William MacDonald who was the first to suggest the idea of such a bibliography and to emphasize the importance of newspapers as historical sources. Most of the reviews of the book picked up this ascription of credit. To my consternation, two months after the book was published, I happened to be reading the *Papers* of the Bibliographical Society of America for 1906, recording the proceedings of the meeting held in Providence in December of that year. One of the papers read at the meeting, and printed in full, was entitled "The Need of a Bibliography of American Colonial Newspapers." It referred to the importance of newspapers as source material, and made a long and urgent plea for a bibliography which would locate all existing files and issues. It suggested that, because of the national scope of the undertaking, the material could best be gathered by an institution which was national in character, such as the American Antiquarian Society. The author of the paper was Clarence S. Brigham, at that time Librarian of the Rhode Island Historical Society. I had completely forgotten that I had ever prepared such a paper or suggested such a project—an unaccountable lapse of memory. Now that I look back upon the plan which I had broached forty-two years ago, I remember that for the next five years I always had the idea in mind and even gathered notes for such a bibliography. I came to Worcester in 1908. In casting around for papers to be read at the annual meeting of the American Antiquarian Society in 1911, I induced Professor MacDonald to include the subject in a paper entitled "Some Bibliographical Desiderata in American History," with which suggestion he complied. His recommendations threw the light of authority upon the undertaking and undoubtedly inspired me to proceed definitely upon the project. The matter of priority as to who suggested the need of a definitive bibliography is not important in itself. I only mention it to record how memory, at least mine, can err. It seems impossible that I could have forgotten my maiden effort in speaking before a national society, but I did.

I have had several opportunities to contribute a paper to some magazine or other upon experiences, social and otherwise, gained from trips covering thousands of miles to the entire eastern half of the country. If I had kept a diary of my travels, this might have been feasible. But I didn't, and the memory of interesting experiences has faded. My primary purpose was to visit a library or a newspaper office, list its early files, and get out as quickly as possible to journey to the next town. I know that in staying at scores of hotels and boarding-houses all over the country, I slept on some hard beds and had some non-nutritious meals. I also remember occasional rebuffs from zealous guardians of files who refused to allow me to examine their newspapers but thought that the catalogue entries were sufficient. In one case I had to wait the entire morning for a custodian to go out to lunch, and then bribed the janitor to let me go to the shelves, where in an hour I completely finished my examination. But the memories of such civic enterprises as roads, transportation systems, hotels, meals, library methods, need of vacuum cleaning of books, attitude toward alcoholic enforcement, etc., have all gone into the limbo of the forgotten. Perhaps it is as well.

The *Bibliography,* after many delays due to the shortage of all-rag paper, the want of compositors and other hindrances, finally was printed and bound late in May 1947. The edition was 1,500 copies. A pre-publication price of $8.00 was set, absurdly low in view of the fact that the cost of the book was double that amount, but it was made possible through a grant of $5,000 from George F. Booth and Harry G. Stoddard, publishers of the *Worcester Telegram* and *The Evening Gazette.* Upon the day of publication the price was advanced to $15.00. There was an original subscription list of 1,200, and nearly 300 copies have since been sold. Only a few copies remain unsold today.

The *Bibliography* contains about one million words and figures. Every word had to be copied once in the original listing, once again in preparing the copy for the printer, and read once in the galley proof and again in the page proof. That made a total of about four million manual and visual operations. The book contained 1,508 pages, of which the index of titles and printers comprised 316 pages. So far almost no errors have been noticed in the printing, although half a dozen omissions in the index have been found. The publication of the *Bibliography* led, as was expected, to the discovery of new and hitherto unlocated files. Issues of the Kittanning, Pennsylvania, *Armstrong True American* in 1813 and the Xenia, Ohio, *Patriot* in 1816, also a file for 1817 of the Petersburg *American Star,* have been located, all of them papers of which no issues were known. Many libraries have acquired new and important issues. As a result a list of additions and corrections will subsequently be printed, recording all such information.

If a personal note has crept into these introductory remarks, it seems unavoidable. The compilation of the *Bibliography* was a lone undertaking, not a summary of what others had written, but the result of personal research. It also seems of possible interest to record the mechanics of preparation and printing, and the history of the project. With this apology, I will take up a few subjects connected with the history of early American newspapers.

History of Early Newspapers

❧❦

THE EARLIEST attempt to prepare a general history of American newspapers was written by John Eliot, librarian of the Massachusetts Historical Society. In the *Collections* of that Society for 1798 and 1799,[1] he contributed "A Narrative of the Newspapers printed in New England." This was in descriptive form, with no tabular listing, and purported to cover New England papers to the Revolution, although it did mention some Philadelphia papers, and in some cases carried the history to a later date. The best record is that of Connecticut, which the author obtained through the assistance of Noah Webster.

The next newspaper history was given by Timothy Alden in his *Glory of America. A Century Sermon,* delivered at Portsmouth in January 1801, and printed in pamphlet form in that year. In an appendix the author furnished a list of New Hampshire newspapers to the end of 1800, a really valuable historical record, as the author had knowledge of facts not obtainable today. This of course was only the record of one state.

---

[1] Vol. V, pp. 208-16; Vol. VI, pp. 64-77.

Noah Webster's interest in newspapers inspired that indefatigable writer to launch a comprehensive project for a history of American newspapers. In June 1801 he sent a printed circular to publishers throughout the country, requesting information about their own newspapers and the papers in their respective localities. Like questionnaires of the present day, the result was not too satisfactory. He received replies from Hanover, Keene, and Walpole in New Hampshire, Brattleboro and Windsor in Vermont, Salem in Massachusetts, Providence in Rhode Island, Albany and Hudson in New York, Trenton in New Jersey, Wilmington in Delaware, Alexandria and Washington in the District of Columbia, Pittsburgh in Pennsylvania, and Lexington in Kentucky. The comparatively small number of replies, several of them unsatisfactory and inadequate, evidently discouraged him and he proceeded no further with the project.[2] John Carter of Providence, thinking that a summary of the number of newspapers published would inspire the federal revenue authorities to legislate a newspaper tax, remarked: "My decided Opinion is, that no *Good* can result from the proposed Publication, and *Evil* may be the Consequence."

The next newspaper historian apparently did not

---

[2] The replies are in the Webster Papers in the New York Public Library and are printed in Allen Walker Read's "Noah Webster's Project for a History of American Newspapers" in *Journalism Quarterly*, XI (September, 1934), 258-75.

share Carter's fears, for his record was one largely of the size of newspaper circulations. This was Samuel Miller, D.D., who published at New York in 1803 a two-volume work entitled *A Brief Retrospect of the Eighteenth Century, containing a Sketch of the Revolutions and Improvements in Science, Arts and Literature during that Period.* His voluminous work included a historical résumé of United States newspaper with critical comments on newspaper publishing of considerable contemporary interest. He summarizes the beginnings of newspapers in the Colonies and then says: "In 1801 more than one hundred and eighty different newspapers were printed in different parts of the United States." In a footnote he continues:

> Of these about *fifteen* are *daily* papers; and supposing 1000 copies of each to be printed, the whole number of copies annually distributed, making due allowance for Sundays, &c. will be about 4,590,000. The number printed *three* times a week is about *nine.* Of these, supposing 800 copies to be on an average stricken off, the amount annually distributed will be 1,080,000. About *twenty-five* are printed *twice* a week. Of these, allowing 800 copies each to be the common number sent abroad, the number annually circulated will be 2,000,000. Finally, about *one hundred and thirty* newspapers are printed *weekly;* and, allowing the number of each published to be 800, the amount of this class annually edited will be 5,408,000. So that the whole number of news-

> papers annually circulated in the United States
> may be estimated at *thirteen millions and
> seventy-eight thousand.* For the sake of being
> rather below than above the mark, say *twelve
> millions.* It will be seen, by comparing this
> with a preceding note, that, while the popula-
> tion of the United States is not more than
> *one-half* of that of Great-Britain, the number
> of newspapers, circulated in the former coun-
> try may be estimated at more than *two-thirds*
> of the number published in the latter.[3]

In an Appendatory Note on page 483 he attacks
the subject again, and this time with further information acquired. He lists all of the newspapers in the
country by state and by town, although giving only
numerical count and not titles. He concludes:
"There are then, in the United States, about 200
newspapers. Of these at least seventeen are printed
daily, seven *three times* a week, thirty *twice* a week,
and one hundred and forty-six *weekly.*"

It seems strange that Dr. Miller's *Brief Retrospect*
is so little known. I asked three historical scholars
about the work, and none had ever heard of it. It is
true that the author gives most of his space to the
science, art, and literature of the Old World, yet
when he does comment on American affairs his observations are instructive, since they represent the
opinions of contemporary scholars. His long chapter
on education in the United States is a notable in-

---

[3] Vol. II, p. 251.

stance and the first comprehensive treatment of the subject. Realizing what this learned author tried to accomplish, it is interesting to read the description of his personality given by James W. Alexander in his *Life of Archibald Alexander,* p. 344. He says:

> Dr. Miller came from the training of city life, and from an eminently polished and literary circle. Of fine person and courtly manners, he set a high value on all that makes society dignified and attractive. He was preeminently a man of system and method, governing himself, even in the minutest particulars, by exact rule. His daily exercise was measured to the moment; and for half a century he wrote standing. He was a gentleman of the old school, though as easy as he was noble in his bearing; full of conversation, brilliant in company, rich in anecdote, and universally admired.

There was an occasional attempt on the part of publishers to list the newspapers of their own states. The *Troy Gazette,* on December 16, 1806, printed a list of 54 New York newspapers, grouping them by political affiliations. Although the editor promised to print the records of other states as they were obtained, apparently no more were published.

Apparently the next historical record of newspapers was in a monthly magazine *Omnium Gatherum,* published at Boston in 1810. The publishers received in March 1810 an article entitled "A List of Newspapers and Periodical Publications in the

United States," which they printed in April 1810.[4] This is a list of 238 newspapers and 25 magazines, with the newspapers, titles only, arranged by states. It is presumably a preliminary printing of Isaiah Thomas' 1810 checklist, which appeared when his book was published in May 1810. Thomas went frequently to Boston and may have allowed this list to be issued with the hope of receiving additions and corrections. It is far less complete than the Thomas list, and without the names of printers and other information.

Isaiah Thomas' *History of Printing in America* appeared in 1810. In his diary Thomas records that he sent the first volume to press on January 4, the second volume on April 24, and that the work was "finished at Press" on August 14. He immediately sent copies to various libraries and friends. There seems to be no record preserved of the cost of the work or the size of the edition. It is so well known that there is no reason to describe it here. Thomas could write such a history better than any printer of his day. His own memory extended back for half a century, he had friendships with all the leading printers, he owned the best existing collection of early American books and newspaper files, and he was imbued with a desire for accuracy and fact, rather than for literary expression. He worked strenuously

---

[4] Vol. I, pp. 251-54.

for three years in compiling the history, visited
Boston frequently to work for hours in collections
and archives, obtained interviews with old-time
printers, inserted advertisements in many newspapers
seeking for information, and conducted a large correspondence to gain new facts. The result was a work
that was invaluable and irreplaceable. There are
faults, chiefly in arrangement, since separate histories of printing and of newspapers caused redun-
dancy and duplication of statement. It is remarkable
that there are so few errors, considering how much
the author had to rely on memory. Some sections are
better covered than others.[5] He once remarked that
the history would have been more complete if he
could have made a journey to the South. It is true,
also, that the narrative carried only to the Revolution, although he partially atoned for this by compiling an exhaustive list of newspapers published in
1810, which contains titles and names of printers not
ascertainable today. That the book is regarded as a
classic in American historical literature is shown by
the fact that it was included in the Grolier Club
exhibit of One Hundred Influential American Books.

---

[5] The history of Philadelphia printing could have been well enlarged.
This is shown by the communications which William McCulloch sent to
Thomas in 1812-15, comprising over three hundred pages of notes and
reminiscences. This interesting, and often important, material was
printed in the American Antiquarian Society *Proceedings* for April 1921,
under the title of "William McCulloch's Additions to Thomas's History
of Printing."

After the publication of Thomas' history there were occasional attempts on the part of publishers to secure complete lists of newspapers and periodicals either for their own states or for the entire country. The most pretentious was that launched by Henry C. Lewis, editor of *The Hive,* of Washington, D. C. In the issue of July 6, 1811, he published the following notice to newspapers throughout the country:

> The Editors of the Hive having commenced, and wishing to complete, a correct List of all Newspapers and periodical and diurnal publications, political, commercial, agricultural, literary, &c. &c. in the United States, take this mode of respectfully calling to their aid all those who may have it in their power to promote the completion of the same; and politely beg the Editors or Printers of all such works to forward a No. or Title, to H. C. Lewis, G. Street, Washington City, D. C., with the city, town, village, or county, and state, in which it may be published, and the name of the editor marked (if not printed) on the same.
>
> It may be necessary to forward 3 or 4 successive nos. by successive mails, as one may miscarry or be lost.
>
> As a compensation for which, a copy of the contemplated work will be forwarded to them as soon as printed.
>
> The printers of the U. States will also increase this favor by inserting the above a few times.[6]

Very few publishers printed his communication,

---

[6] Washington *Hive,* July 6, 1811, in Library of Congress.

so far as I can learn, and doubtless the meager returns forced him to drop his laudable undertaking. A similar project apparently met with a similar fate. The Columbia, S. C., *Telescope* of March 12, 1816, stated that the editors of the Winchester *Kentucky Advertiser* desired the names of all newspapers in the United States, asking printers to send one or more of their respective publications, in return for which they would receive a copy of the completed list. The editors of the Kentucky paper at that time were Nathaniel Patten, Jr., and Nimrod L. Finnell, yet none of the known issues of their paper early in 1816 happens to mention their venture. Again, few papers so far as I can find published their announcement, and they, like their Washington predecessor, became discouraged as newspaper annalists.

The most successful endeavor to obtain lists of newspapers was accomplished through a plan proposed by Hezekiah Niles, editor of *Niles' Weekly Register,* which was suggested to him by the publishers of the Richmond *Compiler.* In his magazine for December 1817, he announced that he desired lists of the newspapers of the country and that at least one editor in each state should send him, for publication, such a list, with names of editors, political character, and size of sheet. With the backing of an important publication he obtained results. Maryland was the first to reply, and its list of 18 papers was

printed in the *Register* of December 27, 1817. In his
issues from January 3 to February 7, 1818, Niles
stated that Virginia, New York, Kentucky, Ohio,
Vermont, and Connecticut had replied, but none of
their lists was printed. Perhaps this was because
such lists were already printed in the newspapers of
the editors who had answered. At least the Virginia
list was presumably printed in the Richmond *Compiler* (not located, however); the New York list appeared in the *Albany Argus* of January 6, 1818; the
Kentucky reply came from the Frankfort *Commen-
tator* (no 1818 file located); the Ohio list was printed
in the Columbus *Ohio Monitor* of January 1, 1818;
the Vermont list appeared in the Brattleboro *American Yeoman* of January 13, 1818; and the Connecticut list appeared in the Hartford *Times* of February
2, 1818. In addition, the list of Pennsylvania newspapers was printed in the *York Gazette* of April 23,
1818. Therefore at least eight states had furnished
lists of their newspapers, and even that showing was
respectable and very important.

It remained for Daniel Hewett to compile in 1828
an exhaustive list of newspapers and periodicals published in the United States. In the June 1828 issue
of his *Traveller and Monthly Gazetteer* Hewett
printed a list of 681 newspapers and 119 magazines,
arranged by states and giving title, place and day of

publication, name of publisher, and subscription price.[7]

It all goes to show that coöperative ventures, depending on the kindness of those who are willing to help, are not so successful as an undertaking engineered by a single compiler.

---

[7] The list was reprinted in American Antiquarian Society *Proceedings* for October 1934.

Titles of Newspapers

❖❖❖

THE TITLES of early newspapers are much the same as they are today or, to state it inversely, present-day publishers follow precedent in continuing the old titles. By far the most common of early titles were "Gazette" and then "Advertiser." Between 1704 and 1820 "Gazette" was used either singly or as a part of newspaper titles 488 times. This was closely followed by "Advertiser" with 440 times, showing the deference which publishers paid to their advertisers who made up the greater part of a newspaper's profit. These two titles were followed by "Herald" with 115 times, "Journal" 114, "Intelligencer" 104, "Register" 86, "Republican" 77, "Chronicle" 75, "Patriot" 57, "Centinel" or "Sentinel" 56, and "Courier" 45. Titles frequently used, but in lesser number, were "Eagle," "Mercury," "Messenger," "Monitor," "Museum," "Observer," "Post," "Recorder," "Repository," "Star" and "Times." Such common present-day titles as "Globe," "World," and "Bulletin" were used only once or twice, and we find before 1820 no mention whatever of "Tribune" or "Transcript." The title "Apollo" was employed nine times, although, amusingly, somewhat later, in 1825, the town of Belvidere, New Jersey, named its paper *The Belvidere Apollo.*

The title of "Telegraph" forms an interesting commentary upon the sudden popularity of names for newspapers. Between 1792 and 1794 several systems of telegraphic signals were developed in England and France. These were chiefly dependent upon cross-bars pivoting into different positions at the top of high poles, notably the system originated by M. Chappe of France. Lights at the top of poles were also used, naval signals through flags were employed, and even the theory of sending electric sparks over a wire was made the subject of experiments. On February 10, 1795, a paper was established at Carlisle, Pennsylvania, entitled *The Telegraphe.* The initial issue presented a history of telegraphic experiments taken from English and French periodicals, and stated that it was the first paper in America to use the title. This was strictly true, but the priority was only by a few days. On March 4, 1795, the *Fells-Point Telegraphe* was established at Baltimore, and during the month three other papers, at Greenfield (Massachusetts), Charleston, and Baltimore, changed their titles so as to include the word *Telegraphe.* In the next five months four more newspapers made the word a part of their titles.

This popularity of the word *Telegraphe* was an American outburst. Two obscure papers in London and in Paris had used the title in 1794, but it was never popular then or in subsequent years. In America, however, forty newspapers before 1821 had employed this significant word. The magnetic telegraph, which meant the sending of messages for long distances over wires, was not developed until 1844, and immediately the gathering of news was revolutionized.

Newspaper *vs.* Magazine

❦❦❦❦❦❦❦❦❦❦❦❦❦❦❦❦❦❦❦❦❦❦❦❦❦❦❦❦❦❦❦❦❦❦❦❦❦

THE DECISION whether a publication is a newspaper or a magazine is frequently difficult to make. Format, frequency of publication, inclusion of current news, and especially the intention of the publisher—all have to be taken into consideration. Yet no one of these can be the governing factor. *The Youth's News Paper,* published at New York in 1797, was a small octavo, distinctly a magazine in appearance, yet it considered itself a newspaper, as evidenced by its title, and summarized the news of the day for younger readers. The Sangerfield, New York, *Civil and Religious Intelligencer* was also an octavo, but featured current and local news. As for periodicity, newspapers, with very few exceptions, were published weekly or oftener. Magazines, although sometimes published weekly, were generally issued monthly or even quarterly.

In my *Bibliography* I took as the test of a newspaper generally the inclusion of current news and of advertisements, realizing, however, that some ostensible and professed magazines occasionally provided such features. Marriage and death records are always an important part of a newspaper's coverage, and perhaps I admitted some border-line publications since they contained such valuable data.

The publisher's intention is an important factor in defining whether a publication is a newspaper or a magazine. Elias Smith stated with regard to his *Herald of Gospel Liberty,* published at Portsmouth, Portland, and Philadelphia between 1808 and 1815, "A religious Newspaper is almost a new thing under the sun; I know not but this is the first ever published to the world." Yet he carried almost no current news, except for religious intelligence, and the contents were chiefly those of a magazine. When Nathaniel Willis started his Boston *Recorder* in 1816 and wished it to be known as the first religious newspaper in the world, the only way he could get around Elias Smith's publication was to call it "a circular" and to add "a proper newspaper is in the folio form."[1] The most striking case of a newspaper calling itself a magazine is Isaiah Thomas' *Worcester Magazine* of 1786-88. Massachusetts passed a state tax on advertisements in newspapers. So Thomas promptly changed his title from *Thomas's Massachusetts Spy* to *Worcester Magazine,* reduced the size from folio to octavo, and then continued the same kind of news that he had published in his newspaper. When the state lifted the tax, he resumed in newspaper form. The *North-Carolina Magazine,* pub-

---

[1] Frederic Hudson, *Journalism in the United States,* p. 293.

lished at Newbern in 1764, was a newspaper in spite of its title.

There is great need of a complete checklist of American magazines, at least to the year 1820, if not to 1830. Frank Luther Mott in his excellent *History of American Magazines* lists 200 magazines from 1741 to 1820, and 302 to 1830. But Mr. Mott's list does not attempt to record locations, which are most valuable to the research worker.

Gaylord P. Albaugh, of McMaster University, Hamilton, Ontario, has been working for several years on a checklist of American religious periodicals from 1730 to 1830, and his latest enumeration shows 640 titles, although because of the interrelationship between titles the list represents 535 distinct journals. It is to be hoped that Mr. Albaugh's bibliography, with its excellent record of locations, will soon be published.

The most pretentious attempt to make early American periodicals of service to research students is that conducted by University Microfilms of Ann Arbor, Michigan. In 1942 they issued a microfilm series completely reproducing all American periodicals, 99 in number, from 1741 to 1799. Following this publication they began upon another series, covering American periodicals, about 500 in number, from 1800 to 1825. They found it necessary to use the resources of seventy-six libraries to complete the series. This project is now under way, and the films from 1800 to 1809 have been completed. The account of the project, with the list of periodicals included, was printed in the *Library Journal* of February 1, 1946.

Although the microfilm series makes the various files of magazines available for use, there is no history of the journals nor any index of printers and publishers. In addition, the high cost of the series makes its acquisition difficult for any but the larger and wealthier libraries. There is great need of a bibliography carrying magazines at least to the year 1830, based upon the same type of information as that contained in the *Bibliography of Newspapers* to 1820, and thus including history, location of files, and an index of titles and printers.

Circulation

❖❖❖❖❖❖❖❖❖❖❖❖❖❖❖❖❖❖❖❖❖❖❖❖❖❖❖❖❖❖❖❖❖❖❖

THE EARLIEST statement about news-
paper circulation in the country was made by John
Campbell in his *Boston News-Letter* of August 10,
1719. In discussing his grievances regarding the costs
of publication, he remarks that "he cannot vend 300
at an Impression, tho' some ignorantly concludes he
Sells upwards of a Thousand." Isaiah Thomas, whose
knowledge of American newspapers extended from
the middle of the eighteenth century until his death
in 1831, remarked:[1] ' ιn 1754, four newspapers only
were printed in New England, these were all published in Boston, and, usually, on a small sheet; they
were published weekly, and the average number of
copies did not exceed six hundred from each press.'
    Circulation gradually grew as the exciting days of
the Revolution approached. Rivington's *New York
Gazetteer* of October 31, 1774, boasted "The weekly
impression of this Gazetteer is lately increased to
thirty-six hundred, a number far beyond the most
sanguine expectations of the Printer's warmest
friends; as the presses of very few, including those in
Great Britain, exceed it." Thomas, according to his

---

[1] *History of Printing* (ed. 1874), II, 8.

statement in the *Massachusetts Spy* of December 21, 1780, had a pre-Revolutionary circulation in Boston of 3,500 copies. Then he was driven out of Boston by the British invasion and established the *Spy* at the small inland town of Worcester. In 1775-76 his circulation was 1,500, in 1778-79 about 1,200, and in 1781 at best but 500. Yet, as Thomas remarked, "It has always been allowed that 600 customers, with a considerable number of advertisements, weekly, will but barely support the publication of a newspaper."

Thomas, on another page of his *History*, said that by 1773 the subscription list of the *Spy* was larger than that of any other newspaper printed in New England. Yet a very few years later he yielded the palm to the *Connecticut Courant* of Hartford. He said:[2]

> After the British troops gained possession of New York, and the newspapers on the side of the country in that place were discontinued, and the printers of them dispersed, the Courant became of much consequence; its circulation rapidly increased; and, for sometime, the number of copies printed weekly was equal to, if not greater, than that of any other paper on the continent.

In the last decade of the eighteenth century the number of newspapers increased, but circulation did not keep step and in general averaged from 600 to 700. A few newspapers of the larger cities stood out,

---

[2] *History of Printing*, II, 62, 90.

such as the *Maryland Journal* of Baltimore which claimed a circulation of "near 2000." Frank L. Mott, in commenting upon circulations in this decade, says:[3]

> The semi-weekly *Columbian Centinel* prob-
> ably topped the list, with over 4000. *Porcu-*
> *pine's Gazette,* a daily, claimed over 2000 early
> in 1799; this was as large a circulation as that
> of any English daily. The *Aurora* in its prime
> had about 1700. Among the country papers,
> the *Farmer's Weekly Museum,* which had some
> 2000 at the height of its popularity, was prob-
> ably the leader.

Circulation was reflected in cost. The three Boston printers of the *Columbian Centinel,* the *Mercury,* and the *Commercial Gazette,* in an effort to stand-ardize their expenses, stated on October 3, 1798, that "the Centinel is published at a weekly expense of 120 Dollars; the Mercury at 80 Dollars; and the Com-mercial Gazette at 50."

Joel Munsell, whose knowledge of newspapers was the widest for the first half of the nineteenth cen-tury, makes several interesting comments on circula-tions in the year 1816: "The number of papers issued by the New York press at that time was as follows:

Mercantile Advertiser	2250
New York Gazette	1750
Evening Post	1600
Commercial Advertiser	1200"

---

[3] *American Journalism* (1941), p. 159.

He continued, "It is remarkable that the Albany
Argus, which was begun by Mr. Buell in 1813, at-
tained a circulation of 4000, the largest in the state,
and had to be put to press the day before its date, it
was said."[4]

Even after 1820, circulation did not notably increase. Michael Chevalier, an observing French
critic, writing of this country in 1834,[5] remarked that

> The American newspapers are very numer-
> ous, but in consequence of their great number
> their circulation is comparatively small. There
> are few daily papers whose circulation exceeds
> 2000, and not one which exceeds 4000; that of
> most of the newspapers is not more than 400 or
> 500. The American newspapers have little re-
> semblance to the French and English. They are
> chiefly mere advertising sheets; they do not
> direct public opinion, they follow it. This local
> character does not allow of their having much
> influence out of their particular district.

It was well after 1850 before greatly increased circulations of 50,000 or over arrived As the country
trebled in population and a greater interest in political affairs spread throughout the nation, and incidentally improved lighting facilities made easier the
reading of newspapers, circulation, especially in the
large cities, expanded and so continued through
the period of the Civil War.

---

[4] *Typographical Miscellany* (1850), annotated copy in American Antiquarian Society, pp. 122c, 232b.
[5] *Society, Manners and Politics in the United States* (1839), p. 452.

Subscription Worries

ONE OF the chief worries of an early newspaper publisher was to collect his subscriptions There was scarcely a newspaper where the printer at one time or another did not refer to this embarrassment. Money was scarce, the newspaper was not a necessity, and too often the printer was lenient. Threats were of little avail, and frequently the subscriptions lagged for years. John Peter Zenger's complaint, voiced in his *New-York Weekly Journal* of February 25, 1751,[1] is but a sample of the publisher's admonition:

> My country subscribers are earnestly desired to pay their arrearages for this Journal, which, if they don't speedily, I shall leave off sending, and seek my money another way Some of these kind customers are in arrears upwards of seven years! Now as I have served them so long, I think it is time, ay and high time too, that they give me my outset; for they may verily believe that my everyday cloathes are almost worn out.

James O'Connor, who published the *Norfolk Herald,* penned an appeal to his subscribers in 1808 which was copied by many other papers. The *New York Herald* of September 24, 1808, remarked: "The following is one of the best dunning advertisements

---

[1] Quoted by Thomas, *History of Printing*, II, 103.

we have ever seen. If the persons to whom it is addressed do not take the hint, they must be very callous," and then proceeded to quote it as follows:

The Printer of the Norfolk Herald to His Subscribers.
Gentlemen,

Saturday next will commence the 5th year of this Establishment.—Your Printer has served an apprenticeship of *seven* years to his trade, and a *double* apprenticeship to the trade of DUNNING! The mysteries of the latter branch are too deep, and the instruments so dull or so delicate, that he almost despairs of producing any *effect*—But it is incumbent on him to be as obliging as possible, and as solicitation appears to be agreeable to many of you, your Printer goes on to gratify your feelings in language that you cannot misconstrue, and that he hopes will continue to please—Some modest persons would say, *can you pay me? Will you pay me? Please pay me?*—But when I ask for my own, for what I have laboriously earned, and for that which you justly owe me, and without which I cannot subsist at all, I am obliged to throw the usual modesty of Printers on the shelf with our other lumber, and say, *you must pay me—my family, my journeymen, my boys, nor even my Devils, not one of them shall starve while one of you owe me, justly owe me a shilling.* 'Tis to delinquents, to your *three* year old, *five* year old non-paying subscribers that the Printer speaks. Did you suppose that he purchased types, paper, ink and hired men for your amusement?—Did you not promise to pay him for his labour?—Have you not received your papers?—Do you never read them?—Do you never blush when you read of

> swindlers, robbers, &c. in the Herald? You per-
> haps consider that you do not belong to the
> class of swindlers, robbers, &c.—To what class
> do you then belong?—To the class of honest
> men truly?—If so, pay the labourer his hire, or
> throw up the paper at once.

This dunning announcement has been quoted at length, since it embodies the feeling which all printers must have felt. Many newspaper publishers went to the wall because they couldn't collect their debts. The *Albany Register* suspended publication on May 13, 1817, not for want of subscribers, but on account of their delinquency. Joel Munsell, the news-paper historian, quotes a satirical reason why sub-scribers would not pay,[2] although I am unable to locate the original reference. He quotes as follows:

> Newspaper publishers make loud complaints
> about the remissness of their patrons, and
> many of them affect to be unable to account
> for so general a thing. It does not seem to have
> occurred to any of the craft that the delin-
> quents aforesaid are universally acquainted
> with the story related by Rabelais of one Philli-
> pot Plact, who being brisk and hale, fell dead
> as he was *paying an old debt*—which doubtless
> deters them from paying theirs, fearing a like
> accident.

Nearly all of the early printers took goods and food in lieu of cash Zenger, in the admonition of 1751 noted above, begs his subscribers to "send the poor printer a few Gammons or some Meal, some

---

[2] *Typographical Miscellany* (1850), p. 128.

Butter, Cheese, Poultry, &c." On October 6, 1778, the printers of the *Connecticut Courant* announced that payment for one year's subscription would be "one bushel and three pecks of Wheat, or two bushels and a half of Rye, or three bushels and a half of Indian Corn, or half a hundred of Flour or a Load of Wood or an equivalent in Cash.'

Elijah Russel, who published *Russel's Echo* at Fryeburg, Maine, thus waxed poetical in his issue of May 17, 1798:

> *Ho! all who thirst for News!*
> *Come, and our sheets peruse:*
> *The Fryeburg Press invites*
> *All, Jews and Israelites.*
> *Payments easy made, in anything you please,*
> *Wheat, rye, corn, butter, pork, flax, cheese;*
> *Cash will not be rejected*
> *Tho' much is not expected.*

The Columbus, Ohio, *Western Intelligencer* of December 10, 1814, thoroughly covered the list of wants as follows:

> Accomodation to Subscribers. The following articles of Country Produce will be received in payment for the newspaper; viz: Beef, pork, flour, Indian corn and meal, oats, butter, cheese, lard, fowls, eggs, sauce of almost any kind, wool, flax, honey, bees-wax, tallow, candles.

The printer, especially of the small country newspaper, had to live, and to him food was as valuable as money.

Advertisements

ADVERTISEMENTS in early newspapers were the chief source of revenue, as it has always been from the beginning to the present day. Noah Webster, writing to Rev. John Eliot in 1798,[1] said: "Merchants alone enable printers to sell their papers low, & they will have their advertisements *displayed*. A literary paper without advertisements would cost fifteen or twenty dollars a year, if daily, & in proportion, if published once or twice a week." The publisher of the *New York Evening Post,* in its issue of December 1, 1803, concisely stated the case for his fellow craftsmen, to cover a period of two centuries: "Subscribers alone, allowing them to be quadruple to what was ever known in this city, would not support a Newspaper establishment; and, in fact, it is the advertiser who provides the paper for the subscriber."

It is the advertisements, furthermore, that provide the local color, and enable the historian to reconstruct the picture of a community far more than all the reading matter in the so-called news. The column of local news was sparse indeed throughout the whole colonial period. It took an event of outstanding importance to earn a place there. A visit from a nation-

---

[1] Letter of Nov. 25, 1798, in Mass. Hist. Soc. Mss. vol. 029,10c.

ally known celebrity, or an exceptional outburst of storm or weather disturbance, or a good murder, a fire, or a startling accidental death would cause such an event to receive a brief notice. But ordinary happenings of interest, such as are chronicled in detail today, were entirely overlooked. Presumably the editor assumed that such incidents would be already known to the citizens and would constitute unnecessary information.

Therefore the advertisements give the detailed picture of social and economic life in the community. The variety is endless. Merchandise such as clothes, clocks, watches, silver, tools, fruits and liquors, auction sales, patent medicines, publication of books, theatrical entertainments, leases and sales of houses and lands, stallions for breeding, runaway slaves and apprentices, sailing of vessels, stage routes, language and music teaching, horse racing, and, as Benjamin Franklin concluded one of his advertisements, others "too tedious to mention." In no place can one better find the story of the cloths and textiles imported from England, India, China, and all over the world than in the lengthy advertisements of the leading merchants. The study of Revolutionary uniforms, for instance, can be made in no other way than by reading the careful descriptions of clothes worn by army deserters.

Advertising began, of course, in a small way. The first advertisement was in the second issue of the

Boston News-Letter, the offer of a reward for the return of two anvils which had been stolen from Mr. Shipen's wharf. For the next thirty years advertising made little increase or display. The advertisements were crowded together on the last page, without dividing lines or headings or anything to make them attractive. It was Benjamin Franklin who gave the subject more of a modern touch. In 1729 he introduced headlines, space between, and better typography. His rival, Andrew Bradford, in the *American Weekly Mercury* also made advertising more attractive at about the same time, in 1730. Several papers preceded Franklin in the use of stock cuts to illustrate their advertisements. From then to the end of the century the art of display continually improved. Advertisements frequently took the space of two columns, and in a few instances an entire page. Andrew Bradford, for instance, used all of the fourth page of the *American Weekly Mercury* of December 28, 1731, to advertise a long list of 172 titles of books for sale. Merchants occasionally took a full page to advertise a vast amount of merchandise, for example, Jolley Allen in the *Boston Gazette* of September 7, 1767.

The amount of advertising gradually increased until in the 1790's some of the mercantile papers of the large cities were devoting from one-half to three-quarters of their four folio pages to advertisements; and often they were required to issue supplements.

A single issue of the *New York Gazette* of January 1, 1818, contained 538 advertisements, comprising twenty-five out of twenty-eight columns. The fact that the word "Advertiser" appeared as part of the title of 440 newspapers before 1821 shows what an influence the subject held in the mind of the publisher.

The cost of advertising increased with the years. The initial issue of the *Boston News-Letter* in 1704 announced that advertisements would cost from 12 pence to 5 shillings, the latter for a paragraph of about twenty lines. Not all printers announced their rates, and undoubtedly the question was subject to bargaining. Presbrey, in his volume on the history of advertising,[2] in commenting on the price asked by some eighteenth-century newspapers, says:

> Zenger's rate for an advertisement was "three shillings for the first week and one shilling every week after." The Virginia Gazette accepted advertisements "of moderate length" at three shillings for the first publication and two shillings for each repeat. The Maryland Gazette's rate was five shillings for first insertion and one shilling for each succeeding insertion. The New Jersey Gazette asked seven shillings six pence for the first and two shillings six pence for repeated insertions.

---

[2] Frank Presbrey, *History and Development of Advertising* (1929), p. 144, an excellent book, made especially useful by its numerous illustrations. This particular paragraph, however, regarding cost of advertising, was taken almost bodily from North's *History of the Newspapers and Periodical Press of the United States* (1884), published as one of the volumes of the U. S. Tenth Census.

The three leading newspaper publishers of Boston in 1798, proprietors of the *Centinel,* the *Mercury,* and the *Commercial Advertiser,* adopted the following uniform rate for advertising:[3] "Two dollars per square (which will measure from 20 to 25 lines) must be paid for; all lengthy advertisements inserted three times, and none, however short, can be admitted for less than 50 Cents; and one sixth part for each continuance after the first three insertions." The Wilmington *Mirror of the Times* in its masthead during 1800 announced as follows: "Advertisements, of no more length than breadth, inserted four times for one dollar, and twenty cents for each succeeding time—larger ones in proportion—liberal deductions made for those inserted by the year." Evidently the papers in the smaller towns charged less for advertising.

Advertisements in general, in spite of the value of the subject matter for historical study, were uninteresting. Occasionally an advertiser would break into rhyme, which enlivened the printed page, whether or not it was successful as a selling argument. Daniel Dod, a Newark surveyor, in planning to remove to another location, thus advertised in the *New York Gazette,* January 6, 1730:

> *Let this give Notice to my Friends,*
> *That I am about to move,*
> *To try to better my Condition,*

---

[3] *Columbian Centinel,* Oct. 3, 1798.

> *As it doth me behove*
> *And if any want that I*
> *Should Land for them survey,*
> *Let them apply themselves to me*
> *Before I go away.*

The Springfield *Hampshire Chronicle* of June 4,
1788, carries a long poetical advertisement, sub-
mitted by Marcus Marble, whose poetry is less notable than his faith in nostrums:

> *Marcus Marble*
> *Has lately receiv'd, and is now very willing,*
> *On terms which are easy, quite soon to be*
>   *selling,*
> *An assortment of medicines, all genuine,*
> *And Drugs which are us'd in the medical line:*
> *Doctor Bateman's grand cordial elixir, for cure*
> *Of disorders of body, so notedly sure;*
> *With his pectoral drops, which are very well*
>   *known*
> *To people residing in country and town;*
> *Doctor Turlington's balsam of life, and the*
>   *best,*
> *Has been proved, and found to be* probatum
>   est;
> *Hooper's, Anderson's, Locker's, and other fine*
>   *pills,*
> *Which often have cur'd the most dangerous*
>   *ills;*
> *Oleum rifini, six shillings per bottle,*
> *And British oil, cheap, if your purses will*
>   *rattle.*
>   *— ALSO —*
> *French brandy, New-England and West-India*
>   *rum,*
> *All which are well pleasing to palates of some;*

Very good Lisbon and Malaga wine,
A glass just before, and one after you dine,
Will raise up your spirits when once they are low,
And remove a disorder that's call'd the hypo.
Molasses, loaf sugar, brown ditto, and tea,
Of an excellent quality, though it's Bohea;
Good coffee, and choc'late, of elegant taste,
Fit either for morning or evening repast; . . .

. . .

All these will be sold very cheap; but no trust
Is allow'd to the best any more than the worst;
In payment is taken Gold, Silver and Cents,
Good country produce, and final settlements.

An even longer rhyme was perpetrated by Samuel Wigton in the Hudson *Bee* of August 23, 1803. It is quoted at length, chiefly to show the vast array of goods carried in a country store:

Samuel Wigton,

Having lately replenished his store
With the following goods, and many more,
Offer them to his friends for sale,
Either by wholesale or retail.
Broadcloths, light, dark, red, blue, brown,
Kerseymeres, coatings, and swansdown,
Velvets, black, olive, strip'd, and plain,
Thicksets, corduroys, fustians, jean,
Silk, color'd and plain nankeen,
Flannels, red, yellow and green,
Men's hose, silk, cotton, worsted, assorted,
Checks and stripes, homemade and imported,
Koram and felt hats, blankets, (rose)
Lion-skins, and ready-made clothes.
ALSO—Lustrings, black, brown and blue,
Pelongs and sarsnets of all Kinds too,

Muslins, color'd, sprigg'd, plain, printed,
Tambour'd, cross-barr'd, ornamented,
Chintzes, calicoes and linens,
Cotton stuffs and yarn for spinning,
Gurrahs, humhums and platillas,
All kinds of bonnets, shawls, unbrellas,
Camlets, durants, black, blue, green,
Calimancoes, russels and moreens,
Cambrics, satins, lawns and laces,
Shalloons and wildbores in their places,
Handkerchiefs, ribbons, threads and tapes,
Silks, twist, millinet and crapes,
Pins, needles, thimbles, bindings, wires,
Fans, gloves and mitts for all desires,
Shoes of all qualities made to suit
The gentleman's, lady's or child's foot.
Wines, brandy fit for any use,
Good high proof rum from Santa Cruse,
Cherry rum, spirits and molasses,
And homemade gin which none surpasses,
Teas, sugars, coffee, chocolate, rice,
Soap, pepper, ginger and alspice,
Best indigo, tobacco, and snuff,
Copperas, alum, brimstone enough,
Brushes, red wood, powder, shot,
Bar lead, paper, and what not.
Iron and steel, good solid metals,
Bake pans, smoothing-irons, pots and kettles,
Locks, pen-knives, razors, Knives and forks,
And tools for all mechanics' works,
Pewter basons, porrengers, platters,
Metal tea-pots and such matters,
Brass headed andirons, shovels and tongs,
Candlesticks, snuffers, pipes short and long,
Copper tea-kettles, Holland skates,
Japann'd waiters, pencils and slates,
Fowling pieces, saw mill saws,

Best steel plated without flaws,
Hollow, stone and crockery ware,
Plaster and clover seed to spare,
And so many more things, large and small,
That a column would not name them all.
Cash or goods are given for wheat,
Rye, corn or any grain to eat:
Oats, flax-seed, anything that way
For the above is taken in pay.

But not all poetical advertisements concerned the sale of merchandise, as witness the following in the Cumberland, Maryland, *Allegany Freeman* of December 11, 1813:

CAUTION

On November the ninth day,
My wife Agnes ran away:
From bed and board did flee, and say
She would no longer with me stay.
But since she left me without cause,
I'll give her time enough to pause,
That she may see her error
When I live happy with a fairer!
Thefore I warn both great and small,
Not to credit her at all:
And for her contracts from this day
Not one farthing will I pay.

GABRIEL KIMMEL

The value of advertisements in the study of social and economic life is evident from an examination of any early American newspaper. Several recent valuable projects in indexing this material by subject have been made and the results issued in printed form. Alfred Coxe Prime of Philadelphia searched the newspapers of Philadelphia, Maryland, and

South Carolina from 1721 to 1800, and copied the advertisements relating to arts and crafts—painting, engraving, silver, pottery, cabinet work, clocks, watches, architecture, and similar subjects. The Walpole Society published the material in two large volumes in 1929 and 1932, and the work has been of inestimable value to students. The portion printed represented only a small part of Mr. Prime's collection of about twénty thousand references, with groups of cards relating to amusements, medicine, printing and bookbinding, ships and shipbuilding, slavery, textiles, and other subjects—all of which material is now in the custody of Mrs. Prime.

George Francis Dow performed a similar task in abstracting the advertisements in the pre-Revolutionary Boston newspapers by producing in 1927 his *Arts & Crafts of New England, 1704-1775,* covering practically the same subjects as Mr. Prime. The New York Historical Society in 1938 issued a large volume of 450 pages entitled *The Arts and Crafts in New York, 1726-1776,* which abstracted the advertisements in New York newspapers and included an even larger number of crafts and trades than those enumerated in the previous compilations. Phases of colonial life other than those treated in the three abovementioned works could well be made the basis of future volumes, and would thus provide an increased knowledge of the ways in which our ancestors lived.

Illustration

UNDER THIS HEADING is taken up all designs and representations, outside of printers' ornaments known as "flowers." The earliest illustration in an American newspaper is that of a flag—a woodcut in the *Boston News-Letter* of January 26, 1708. The article prints a proclamation of Queen Anne declaring what ensigns or colors should be carried by British merchant vessels. It is accompanied by a drawing of a flag about two inches wide, describing by lettering the red background and the crossing of blue and white stripes in the upper left canton. It is evidently the work of a Boston woodcut engraver, faithfully copying a design in the *London Gazette* of August 11, 1707, accompanying the printing of a proclamation by Queen Anne dated July 28, 1707. I have seen the original broadside proclamation in the collection of Lord Crawford in England, and the Antiquarian Society has the *London Gazette*.

The earliest ornamental designs were the woodcut devices used in the headings of newspapers. The *News-Letter* possessed no such device for over half a century. The *Boston Gazette,* established December 21, 1719, the second American newspaper (by one day), adopted two cuts in its heading, one a ship under full sail and the other a galloping postrider blowing his horn. They were both good woodcuts, excellently drawn. The *Gazette* frequently changed its devices. John Boydell, who was postmaster, published the *Boston Gazette* from 1732 to 1734. Late in 1734 he was succeeded as postmaster by Ellis Huske, who immediately established the *Boston Post-Boy*. When Huske adopted similar devices of a full-rigged ship and a galloping postboy, Boydell in October 1734 replaced his postrider with a pine tree. In later years, before the Revolution, the *Gazette* changed its devices to include an Indian, Britannia, and Minerva.

The *American Weekly Mercury* was established by Andrew Bradford at Philadelphia, December 22, 1719. At first it carried no device, but on May 19, 1720, it adopted woodcuts of a postrider and a winged Mercury. They were rather crude and, becoming worn, were redrawn July 16, 1724. On September 11, 1740, Bradford obtained what was probably the best-drawn cut in any colonial newspaper. It took the full width of the page, with a figure of Mercury at the left, a postrider at the right, and in the center a view of Philadelphia, certainly one of the earliest engraved views of that city. It was later used in the *American Magazine* in January 1741. This entire device was used by the *Mercury* to the last issue

NEW-ENGLAND N° 5.

THE
BoftonGazette.

Publifhed by Authority.

From MONDAY January 11. to MONDAY January 18. 1719.

No. 22

THE
AMERICAN
Weekly Mercury,

THURSDAY May 19th, 1720.

Numb. 13.

THE
New-York Gazette.

From February 28. to Monday March 7. 172;-6.

OCTOBER 11. 1735. NUMB. 565.

The Pennfylvania GAZETTE.

Containing the frefheft Ad- ices Foreign and Domeftick.

known, in 1746, although the cuts became much worn.

The *New York Gazette,* established late in 1725, followed custom by having two devices in its heading. One was the inevitable postrider, and the other the New York colony seal, both crudely executed. Many other papers adopted devices in their titles before the Revolution, employing ships, Indians, the royal arms, and similar emblems, but only the earliest have here been noted.

The word "woodcut" has been used in the above paragraphs, and perhaps rather loosely. It is well possible that some of these cuts were cut on metal instead of wood. None of the writers on printing or the chronicles of printing history discuss this difference between engraving on wood or metal, so far as it concerns the use of cuts in America in the first half of the eighteenth century. The best discussion of the subject, I believe, is in Lawrence Wroth's *American Woodcuts and Engraving, 1670-1800,* Providence, 1946, page 12, where he comments on the engravings in Boston publications of 1717-1719 as follows:

> The designation of the supposed James Franklin engravings and several others in the list as "relief cuts" instead of "woodcuts" suggests a conviction of the compilers, supported by a number of outside opinions, that these Franklin prints, and doubtless many more of

ILLUSTRATION 41

the period, were metal cuts in the woodcut
manner, made with a graver upon pewter or
copper rather than with a knife on a plank
surface.... Once the distinction between woodcuts and metal cuts in relief has been set up in
the observer's mind he finds many things to
convince him that the metal cut procedure was
fairly common in the colonies and that many
illustrations commonly described as woodcuts
are in reality metal cuts in the woodcut manner. In some of the cruder productions, illustrated broadsides, for example, it is possible to
see in the borders of the prints the heads of the
nails which fastened the metal plate to a wood-
block for the impression. Despite the fact that
it is frequently very difficult to say whether a
print has been made from a woodcut or from
a metal cut in relief, the distinction between
the two processes is of interest in the history of
engraving.

Illustrations or designs in the text of newspapers
were very few before the Revolution. Following the
portrayal of the English merchant flag of 1708, there
was no other illustration, so far as I have discovered,
until 1733, when Zenger's *New York Weekly Journal*
in its issue of December 24 reproduced in a line cut
a map of Louisbourg. This was designed from memory by a Boston mariner, John Gardner, who visited
Louisbourg in October 1733, and upon his return to
Boston directed how it should be drawn. Since the
English were jealous of the activities of the French
in Canada, Zenger gave up most of two issues of his

paper to the subject of Louisbourg. In the following year the *American Weekly Mercury* of October 17, 1734, printed in type a large design comprising the "Order of Battle of the French Army in the Lines before Phillipsburg, in Case of an Attack by the Germans." An explanatory note states: "This, if the Print would have permitted, should have been done circularly, like a Half-Moon."

Franklin, during the early years of the *Pennsylvania Gazette,* employed no illustrative ideas except in advertisements. In the "Yearly Verses" which he printed, however, he used an excellent woodcut of the Zodiac in 1739, 1740, and 1741. For the Verses of 1743 he devised a portrayal of Father Time, and for 1748 an ornamental design to commemorate the seasons. It is possible that Franklin himself engraved these cuts. In his *Autobiography,*[1] under the year 1727, in referring to his printing-house, he says: "I also engraved several things, on occasion."

Akin to illustrations in the earliest American newspapers were the elaborate initial letters, called "factotums" in the trade. The *American Weekly Mercury* used them as early as January 31, 1721. The *Boston News-Letter* began to use them January 8, 1722, and employed different designs for different letters. They were used sparingly, however, after 1726. Early in 1734 this paper obtained a series of

---
[1] *Select Works* (1856), p. 164.

ILLUSTRATION 43

largc, elaborate factotums, showing a postrider, ship, dove, and angel. The *New York Gazette* used ornamental initial letters in October 1728, the *Pennsylvania Gazette* in March 1731, and the *Boston Gazette* in November 1732. The custom had previously been employed in British newspapers, although the English journals were generally not so interested in ornament or illustration as their American cousins.

A form of illustration in early newspapers was the advertising device. They were, however, not designs cut by local engravers, but cuts generally in type metal imported from English typefounders, like "flowers," as the border printer's ornaments were called. Strangely, designs in advertisements were seldom used in early London newspapers, and in fact they were minimized well throughout the eighteenth century. But the American newspaper publishers sought to brighten their advertisements, dull as they were, in the first half of the century. In the *Boston Gazette,* as early as November 20, 1732, form cuts in advertising were employed, followed by the *Boston News-Letter* and the *American Weekly Mercury* in August 1733, the *Pennsylvania Gazette* in May 1734, the *New York Gazette* in March 1735, and the *South Carolina Gazette* in June 1735. Invariably the first cuts were ships, and gradually designs of houses, books, negroes, and furnishings were used.

The *Pennsylvania Gazette,* during Franklin's early

proprietorship, used cuts in advertisements sparingly. Previous to 1756 it showed almost nothing but cuts of ships accompanying notices of sailings. In 1756 he devised an upholstery advertisement of a sofa surmounted by a crown, and a hand with a pen for a teacher who included penmanship in his schooling. In 1758, advertisements of saddles, spectacles, and mustard jars were illustrated by cuts. Thereafter designs were only occasional, although interesting pictures of stagecoaches were used in the 1760's. Other newspapers also used advertising cuts sparingly. One of the most interesting, because it was an interior view, was that of a man playing an organ, illustrating the advertisement of John Sheybli in the *New York Gazette and Weekly Mercury* of October 10, 1774.

Scarcity of paper, just before the Revolution, undoubtedly tended to prevent overelaboration of advertisements and the waste of needed space. Yet if the merchant wished to spend the money, large and ornamental advertisements could be printed, certainly in the supplements. The device of elaborated borders was occasionally employed after 1760, but it remained for Gerardus Duyckinck, the New York merchant, to develop the handsomest advertisement of colonial times. In issues of the *New York Gazette and Weekly Mercury* from 1767 to 1769 he frequently showed a long announcement of goods for

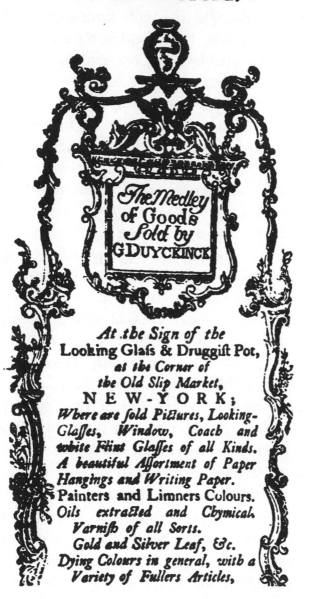

*The Medley
of Goods
Sold by*
G. DUYCKINCK

At the Sign of the
Looking Glass & Druggist Pot,
*at the Corner of
the Old Slip Market,*
N E W - Y O R K ;
*Where are sold Pictures, Looking-
Glasses, Window, Coach and
white Flint Glasses of all Kinds.
A beautiful Assortment of Paper
Hangings and Writing Paper.*
Painters and Limners Colours.
*Oils extracted and Chymical,
Varnish of all Sorts.
Gold and Silver Leaf, &c.
Dying Colours in general, with a
Variety of Fullers Articles,*

sale, half the length of a column, enclosed in a scroll-
work border similar to the trade cards engraved by
Dawkins and Revere. In a shield at the top was the
heading "The Medley of Goods sold by G. Duyckinck," and his shop was "At the Sign of the Looking Glass & Druggist Pot." Although this cut was
drawn by an excellent engraver, most of the advertising cuts throughout the century were stock cuts imported from England. In the Antiquarian Society's
collection of type specimen books, gathered by Isaiah
Thomas, is a copy of Edmund Fry's *Specimen of
Metal Cast Ornaments,* London, 1793. This includes
an impressive array of cuts of ships, horses, dogs,
houses, urns, tea-canisters, musical instruments, initial letters, *finis* designs, etc. Earlier English typefounders carried a lesser stock of such ornaments,
and Caslon for instance in his large *Specimens of
Printing Types* of 1763 includes only "flowers."

To return to illustrative material in newspapers,
the *New York Weekly Post-Boy* of June 10, 1745,
contained a cut, probably on type metal, of a "Plan
of the Town and Harbour of Louisburg." In the
New York Gazette (Weyman's), of December 10,
1759, was printed a cut of the town of Quebec, a
fairly large cut, 6 by 3½ inches, with a series of references to lettered localities on the plate. The colonists
were evidently interested in Canadian affairs.

Benjamin Franklin, in the *Pennsylvania Gazette*

ILLUSTRATION 47

of May 9, 1754, published what may well be called the earliest American newspaper cartoon. In 1754, at a time when the prospect of a war with the French was imminent, a congress of the colonies was called at Albany to be held in June. Franklin, in a plea for united action, published an article on the situation on May 9, accompanied by a cut of a snake divided in eight parts—New England, New York, New Jersey, Pennsylvania, Maryland, Virginia, North Carolina, and South Carolina, and for some reason omitting Georgia. Under the snake was the motto "Join, or Die." The device, which took up the width of a column on the second page, immediately attracted public attention and was reproduced in at least five newspapers and notices in others. The device was so unusual and interesting that it would be worth while to chronicle the details of the various reproductions in newspapers, were it not for the fact that an exhaustive article on the subject was contributed to volume 11 of the *Publications of the Colonial Society of Massachusetts,* in December 1907, by the late Albert Matthews, with an array of notes and photographic reprints of all the varying cartoons. The snake device was of great importance in calling the attention of the colonists to the necessity of union, and was revived at the time of the Stamp Act controversy in 1765 and again during the movement toward independence in 1774. Isaiah Thomas, on July 7, 1774, used the device the full width of the first page in his *Massachusetts Spy,* and added a dragon, representing Great Britain, facing the snake. But, as noted above, there is no need of repeating the information so fully included in Mr. Matthews' monograph. The only addition is to clear up his confusion as to the place of printing of the *Constitutional Courant* of September 21, 1765, which newspaper (or broadside) reproduced the snake device during the Stamp Act troubles. The details of the publishing of this paper, which was printed at Woodbridge, N. J., is told in a letter from William Goddard to Isaiah Thomas, dated April 22, 1811, correcting certain statements in Thomas' *History of Printing.* Since this letter, and a following letter of no date, have never been printed and since they contain first-hand information from an authority who probably knew more than anyone, except Thomas himself, about pre-Revolutionary printers, they are reproduced in a subsequent place in this volume.

Illustrations in American newspapers for the decade preceding the Revolution were scarce. The *Pennsylvania Journal* of October 31, 1765, issued a striking protest against the Stamp Act by printing its first page in imitation of a tombstone, with mourning borders, skull and cross-bones, and the motto: "Expiring: In Hopes of a Resurrection to Life again." This pictorial evidence of opposition to the Stamp

ILLUSTRATION 49

Act had much effect throughout the colonies and helped to unite public opinion.

A few other illustrations may be noted. The *New York Gazette or Post-Boy* of June 12, 1769, the *New York Gazette and Mercury* of June 12, 1769, the *New York Journal* of June 29, 1769, and the *New York Chronicle* of June 15 and 22, 1769, carried line cuts of the transit of Venus, accompanying articles on the subject. The transit occasioned much interest in this country, resulting in printed accounts of the observations made by John Winthrop at Cambridge and Benjamin West at Providence. The *Connecticut Courant* of July 16, 1770, displayed a cut of a comet, which was signed with the initials of "N.S.," undoubtedly Nehemiah Strong, who was then Professor of Mathematics at Yale. The most notable newspaper illustration of the period was the cut of four coffins drawn by Paul Revere for the *Boston Gazette* of March 12, 1770, to commemorate the victims of the Boston Massacre. In the issue of April 20, 1775, the *New York Gazetteer* carried a woodcut of the hanging in effigy of James Rivington.

After the Revolution there was no notable increase in newspaper illustrations. There were the usual advertising cuts, but little departure from previous standards. There seemed to be no particular desire on the part of newspaper publishers to capture the imagination of their readers by inserting pictorial features. One variation, however, was conceived by Benjamin Russell, the enterprising publisher of the *Massachusetts Centinel*. A strong Federalist, he did all in his power to effect the ratification of the Federal Constitution. After eleven states had ratified, and only two—North Carolina and Rhode Island—were outside the fold, he printed in his paper on August 2, 1788, a sizable cartoon which attracted general attention, and must have had some influence. He had a sketch engraved entitled "The Federal Edifice," showing eleven pillars—the states which had ratified —supporting the "National Dome," with one pillar half raised, North Carolina "Rise it will," and another tottering pillar, Rhode Island, "The foundation good, it may yet be saved." A poem underneath began:

> *Eleven Stars, in quick succession rise—*
> *Eleven columns strike our wond'ring eyes,*
> *Soon o'er the whole, shall swell the beauteous*
> *   Dome,*
> *Columbia's boast—and Freedom's hallow'd*
> *   home.*

It seems strange that some effort was not made to use caricature, as the reading matter constantly invited pictorial interpretation. It remained for the political animosities prevalent before the War of 1812 to suggest what was probably the most notable cartoon in early newspaper history. In the bitter struggle between the Democrats and the Federalists for the control of Massachusetts, the former held the

ILLUSTRATION 51

upper hand in 1811, and had elected Elbridge Gerry as Governor. Early in 1812 they sought to strengthen their position by redistricting the towns in Essex County in order to obtain a Democratic majority in the Senate. This flagrant political move was strongly opposed by the Federalists. The *Boston Gazette,* a vigorous Federal paper, in its issue of March 26, 1812, published a cartoon showing the towns of Essex County so arranged that they resembled a monstrous dragon, with wings, claws, and a ferocious head. The Boston *Repertory* of March 27, 1812, reproduced the cartoon, apparently from the identical type-metal cut.

Now the story of the origin of the cartoon becomes obscure. Joseph T. Buckingham, in his *Specimens of Newspaper Literature,* 1852, vol. 2, p. 91, relates that Benjamin Russell, proprietor of the *Centinel,* hung in his office a map of those towns in Essex County which were to compose the new district. One day Gilbert Stuart, the celebrated painter, happened in, looked at the map, and said that it resembled some monstrous animal. He then took a pencil, added a few touches, and said: "There, that will do for a salamander." Russell looked up and said: "Salamander! call it Gerrymander!"

Samuel Batchelder, in a memorandum said to have been written at the time but repeated in more detail in 1873,[2] said that the map of Essex County "was

---

[2] *N. E. Hist. Geneal. Register,* XLVI (1892), 375.

drawn by Nathan Hale, who with Henry Sedgwick were editors of the Weekly Messenger. It was printed in that paper March 6, 1812." Mr. Batchelder goes on to say that later at a party, Mr. Tisdale, the artist, sketched in some wings and made the map into a frightful dragon, also that it was a Mr. Alsop who suggested the name of Gerrymander. The only trouble about this statement is that Nathan Hale was not an editor of the *Messenger* until 1815. There was no Mr. Alsop living in Boston at the time, but of course he may have been a visitor.

James S. Loring, in his *Hundred Boston Orators,* 1852, p. 559, says that the caricature appeared in the *Boston Gazette* in March 1812, that the engraving of the cut was executed by E. Tisdale, and that the "engraving" was first exhibited in the *Centinel* office. Washington Allston, who was calling at the office with James Ogilvie, a lecturer on oratory, noticing the figure, said to Benjamin Russell "it looks like a Salamander." Ogilvie quickly said "Why, let it be named Gerrymander, for the governor." Loring adds that he had this story on the authority of Dr. Joseph Palmer, who had the statement from Benjamin Russell. Ogilvie was an English scholar who lectured extensively in America.

William Dunlap, in his *History of the Arts of Design,* 1834, vol. 2, p. 45, in his sketch of Elkanah Tisdale, says: "He is the author of the political satire

ILLUSTRATION 53

called the Gerrymander, and made designs for it."

Although the weight of authoritative opinion is on the side of Tisdale as the originator of the cut, there are at least three claimants for the honor of inventing the word "Gerrymander." At any rate the word became a part of the English language, and has been used countless times to denote redistricting of communities for political advantage, or even for political deception in general. Most of the histories and dictionaries used the Buckingham reference, which was probably the only one with which they were familiar, although to my mind it is the least credible.

The cartoon rankled in the minds of the Democrats and a year later, at the time of a Federalist victory, some newspapers carefully noted the death of the monster. The *Salem Gazette,* on March 30 and April 2, 1813, reproduced the old cartoon, and then in the issue of April 6, 1813, printed a small cut of a skeleton of the monster, with the words "Hatched 1812, Died 1813." The *Boston Gazette* also, on April 15, 1813, printed a similar small cut, but with the skeleton enclosed in the black borders of a coffin.

All of the newspaper illustrations so far were drawn for political or educational purposes Comic illustrations, which were so highly developed later in the century, were not used until some publications designed chiefly to amuse were started in Boston in

1811-12. These were on the border line between newspapers and magazines. The *Scourge* was established in August 1811, and ran for about four months, to be succeeded by the *Satirist,* which lasted for four months in 1812. They throve on scandal and were sued for libel. A few woodcuts of comic figures were shown in each paper, the same cuts being frequently used. It remained for a paper called the *Idiot or Invisible Rambler,* published in Boston in 1818, to attain the high-water mark for genuine caricature. The name of the editor was given as "Samuel Singleton," which was the pseudonym of Henry Trumbull, whose main purpose was to publish a paper devoted to humor. Trumbull was a Connecticut product who had previously published in 1810 a *History of the Discovery of America,* which pseudohistory subsequently went through many editions. In the *Idiot* he printed humorous tales, such as "My Grandmother, or Tales of New England," "The Sea Serpent," "Western Emigration," and "Journal of Br. Jerry's Tour to the Ohio"—all illustrated with comic drawings. He ridiculed emigration to western states, and the subject was so popular that he issued his articles in pamphlet form in 1819, under the title of *Western Emigration.* I would believe that his series of comic drawings in the *Idiot* was the first of its kind among American newspapers.

The Time-Lag in News

◆◆

For nearly a century and a half after
the establishment of American newspapers, the delay
in receiving news of world events was far beyond the
province of the publisher to control. Kings could
die, battles be fought, and treaties be signed, and it
would be weeks and months before the people whose
lives were affected could know of such events The
news of the death of Queen Anne, on August 1, 1714,
arrived in America on September 15. George I died
June 14, 1727, but his subjects in America did not
learn of it until August 13. George II died October
25, 1760, and it was two months later before the news
arrived at Boston. The signing of the Treaty of Ver-
sailles at Paris on September 3, 1783, providing for
the settlement of the American Revolution, was first
heard of at Boston on October 22, from a vessel
thirty-six days out of London, and it was October 30
before the text was published.

Ocean travel was dangerous, and speed was dependent on the weather. Then too, foreign wars and
privateering made voyages doubly hazardous. When
the *Boston News-Letter* was established in 1704 the
colonies were in the midst of Queen Anne's war and

most of the vessels waited for convoys which generally made for Barbados or Jamaica, and then spread
out for the Atlantic coast-line. The first issue of April
24, 1704, carried London news of December 20, 1703,
four months earlier. Ships might load their passen-
gers and their London newspapers, and then wait
around in the Channel for three weeks or more before sailing. Occasional voyages were faster, when
ships sailed direct or had good weather. For instance,
the issue of June 26, 1704, records a voyage from
England in eight weeks, and on November 20, 1704,
was noted the arrival of a brigantine from Plymouth
in seven weeks. During the first two years of newspaper publication there were exceptional voyages of
six weeks and even five weeks, but the average was
about two months.

An examination of the newspapers of the eighteenth century shows that there was but little improve-
ment in the speed of ships before 1800. In 1785, for
instance, a recording of about fifty voyages shows an
average of seven weeks for the voyage from England.
After the Revolution and before the year 1820 the
merchants began to build larger vessels, which meant
improved speed. In 1820 there were frequent sailings of twenty-eight and thirty days, although storms
and calms necessitated voyages of fifty days and over.
With the coming of the fast packets, the clipper ships,
and steam, speed rapidly improved, but this later
period is outside of the present line of inquiry.

The numerous diaries of travelers who journeyed across the Atlantic show more exactly the speed of passages. In 1722 Samuel Johnson voyaged from Boston to England in thirty-nine days. Benjamin Franklin in returning from England to Philadelphia in 1726 had a rather tempestuous voyage which consumed sixty-seven days. William Beverley sailed from Virginia to Liverpool in thirty-seven days. Samuel Davies traveled from Philadelphia to England in 1753 in the fast time of thirty-five days. Rev. John Tyler sailed from New York to London in 1768 in thirty days, although the return passage took forty-two days. Abigail Adams, whose story of a voyage is one of the most detailed on record, sailed from America to England in thirty days in 1784. These are only a few of the records of crossings taken from the diaries of early travelers;[1] but such records show only the time consumed in sailing from shore to shore, and do not include the days wasted in delay in sailing or in taking on and delivering mail.

Communication throughout the colonies in the eighteenth century was very slow, especially in winter. It took postriders a week to travel from New York to Boston, at least two days from Philadelphia to New York, and a fortnight or more to reach the Southern states. When stagecoaches came into general use about 1785, the delivery of letters and newspapers was speedier and more consistent. A good

---

[1] See William Matthews, *American Diaries* (1945), p. 383.

example of the slowness of mails is revealed by a study of the printing in the colonial newspapers of the Declaration of Independence. This was passed at Philadelphia on July 4, 1776, and was first printed in the *Pennsylvania Evening Post* of July 6. Three days later it was printed in Baltimore and four days later in New York. An examination of all of the newspapers of July 1776 shows the following schedule of printings of this important document. Of course it should be remembered that the printing often had to await the proper day of the newspaper's publication, although a few of the papers published "extraordinary" issues.

Declaration of Independence
Newspaper Printings

July 6 Philadelphia, *Pennsylvania Evening Post*

July 8 Philadelphia, *Dunlap's Pennsylvania Packet*

July 9 Philadelphia, *Pennsylvanischer Staatsbote*

July 9 Baltimore, *Dunlap's Maryland Gazette*

July 10 Philadelphia, *Pennsylvania Gazette*

July 10 Philadelphia, *Pennsylvania Journal*

July 10 Baltimore, *Maryland Journal*

July 10 New York, *Constitutional Gazette*

July 11 *New York Packet*

July 11 *New York Journal*

July 11 Annapolis, *Maryland Gazette*

July 12 New London, *Connecticut Gazette*

July 13 Philadelphia, *Pennsylvania Ledger*

July 13   *Providence Gazette*
July 15   *New York Gazette*
July 15   Hartford, *Connecticut Courant*
July 15   *Norwich Packet*
July 16   Exeter, *New Hampshire Gazette, Extraordinary*
July 16   Salem, *American Gazette*
July 17   Worcester, *Massachusetts Spy*
July 17   New Haven, *Connecticut Journal*
July 18   Boston, *Continental Journal*
July 18   Boston, *New England Chronicle*
July 18   *Newport Mercury, Extraordinary*
July 19   Newburyport, *Essex Journal*
July 19   Williamsburg, *Virginia Gazette* (Purdie) extract; in full July 26.
July 20   Williamsburg, *Virginia Gazette* (Dixon & Hunter)
July 20   Portsmouth, *Freeman's Journal*
July 22   Watertown, *Boston Gazette*

The above list, compiled for the first time, includes every American newspaper published in July 1776, except for the *Germantowner Zeitung,* no issues of which are known for that month. It is of additional interest to note that the Declaration was briefly mentioned in the *London Chronicle* of August 13, 1776, and was printed in full on August 17.

This time-lag in news seems far removed from later forms of communication. With the establishment of the magnetic telegraph in 1844, and the laying of the Atlantic Cable in 1858 (although not perfected until 1866), news was transmitted from country to country instantaneously.

Editorial Scurrility

ONE OF the objectionable features of early American journalism was the scurrility which occasional publishers visited upon rival editors or political adversaries. It was not general, and the few who indulged in such practices were outstanding because of this transgression from decency. Such words as "liar," "traitor," "scoundrel," "rapscallion," "villain," "reptile," "reprobate," "knave," and "blackguard" were used to describe the qualities of one's opponent. Political passions ran high, and not even those in exalted office escaped. There was no bar to such conduct except the law of libel, and when both parties indulged in vituperation there were seldom counter-suits.

In the earlier periods of journalism there were occasional examples of scurrility, generally in letters to the editor Franklin, in his *Autobiography* under the year 1733, writes: "In the conduct of my newspaper, I carefully excluded all libelling and personal abuse, which is of late years become so disgraceful to our country." But with the establishment of the United States, and the beginning of party politics, editorial columns soon became loosened to vituperation and calumny.

Washington was elected president without opposition. Early in his first term the Federalists found that a certain faction of the people did not agree with their views, especially concerning the attitude toward England and France. A new party, at first called the Anti-federalists, and later Republicans, Democrats, Republican Democrats, and even Jacobins, came into being, and the struggle for control was on. The Federalists owned nearly all the newspapers. Therefore the Democrats began to establish important journals in the larger cities. Between 1791 and 1795, Freneau's *National Gazette* and Bache's *Aurora* were established at Philadelphia, and Greenleaf's *Argus* at New York. The *Independent Chronicle* was already flying the Republican flag at Boston. The editors of these papers immediately began to indulge in partisan bitterness. Bache was the leader in opposition to the administration, and his intemperate abuse was largely copied in other Republican papers. Abigail Adams, in writing a letter to her sister in 1797, said that he had "the true spirit of Satan, for he not only collects the billingsgate of all the Jacobin papers, but he adds to it the lies, falsehoods, calumny and bitterness of his own."[1] His attack on Washington, whom the *Aurora* denounced

---

[1] *New Letters of Abigail Adams* (1947), p. 96.

as the "man who is the source of all the misfortunes of our country," is the greatest blot on Bache's reputation. Yet Westcott, the historian of Philadelphia, gave this version of the incident: "According to the late Col. Robert Carr, the article in the *Aurora* was written by Dr. William Reynolds. . . . It was published during the absence from the city of the editor, Mr. Bache, who, on his return, expressed great anger and annoyance at its appearance in the columns of the *Aurora*."[2]

Soon after Jefferson's election and the victory of the Republicans in 1800, Republican papers sprang up all over the country, in small towns as well as large. The old-fashioned idea of a printer starting a newspaper as an adjunct to his printing-shop was forgotten. Papers were established for partisan motives and to further the political aspirations of the office-seekers who sponsored them Scurrility and vilification became commonplace and, now that the Republicans were in power, the Federalist newspapers descended to the most improper forms of abuse, attacking Jefferson without mercy or regard for truth.

James Thomson Callender, an English refugee and scandalmonger, who had previously sided with Jefferson when writing for the Richmond *Examiner,* became editor of the Richmond *Recorder* in 1802 and turned against his old friend, circulating wild stories

---

[2] Joseph Jackson, *Encyclopedia of Philadelphia,* I, 206.

about Jefferson's personal life. His newspaper was a vehicle for many of the lies about public persons spread throughout the country. Nor was his language always choice. Of a political opponent, in his issue of January 12, 1803, he remarked, "he is not only a coward, he is not only an assassin behind the back, but he is a notorious fibber." The word "fibber" was mild for Callender.

William Coleman was selected by Alexander Hamilton and his friends to be editor when they established the New York *Evening Post* in 1801. In his initial issue of November 16, Coleman declared explicitly: "We never will give currency to any thing scurrilous, or indecent, immoral, or profane, or which may contravene the essential principles of social order." But the insolent attacks upon Federalist doctrines inflicted by the Republican newspapers, especially Cheetham's *American Citizen* and Duane's *Aurora,* soon made him forget his promises and fight his opponents with their own weapons. He called Cheetham a "base wretch" and Duane a "low bred foreigner." His well-known satirical poem began: "Lie on, Duane, lie on for pay, and, Cheetham, lie thou too."

The invective displayed in this newspaper war certainly debased the standards of journalism. At Hudson, New York, an editor named Harry Croswell established in 1802 a paper called *The Wasp,* to combat another Hudson paper called *The Bee*. Although Croswell's paper lasted only a few months, it became noted for the vigor of its abuse and the maliciousness of its attacks on Jefferson. Strangely, Croswell spent the last forty years of his life in the ministry. But to chronicle all the newspapers which indulged in scurrility in the first decade of the century would constitute quite a task. Let the manifestation be charged up to the excitement of politics which, to the exclusion of other matters, pervaded the minds of the people.

American observers were cognizant of the low state into which many newspapers had fallen. The *Washington Monitor,* in its issue of August 23, 1808, said:

> It is full time that some effort should be made to purify the presses of the United States, from their froth, their spume, and their coarse vulgarisms. Newspapers of all descriptions teem with bombastic invective, with ridiculous jargon, and empty declamation. The popular taste becomes vitiated, and is prepared to receive the pestilential banquet of every noxious creature that wields a pen or controls a press.

Dr. Samuel Miller's *Brief Retrospect of the Eighteenth Century,* published at New York in 1803, thus summarizes the situation:

> Too many of our Gazettes are in the hands of persons, destitute at once of the urbanity of gentlemen, the information of scholars, and the principles of virtue. To this source, rather than to any peculiar depravity of national

character, we may ascribe the faults of American newspapers, which have been pronounced by travellers, the most profligate and scurrilous public prints in the civilized world. These considerations, it is conceived, are abundantly sufficient to account for the disagreeable character of American newspapers. In every country the selfish principle prompts men to defame their personal and political enemies; and where the supposed provocations to this are numerous, and no restraints are imposed on the indulgence of the disposition, an inundation of filth and calumny must be expected. In the United States the frequency of Elections leads to a corresponding frequency of struggle between political parties; these struggles naturally engender mischievous passions, and every species of coarse invective; and, unhappily, too many of the conductors of our public prints have neither the discernment, the firmness, nor the virtue to reject from their pages the foul ebullitions of prejudice and malice. Had they more diligence, or greater talents, they might render their Gazettes interesting, by filling them with materials of a more instructive and dignified kind; but wanting these qualifications, they must give such materials, accompanied with such a seasoning, as circumstances furnish. Of what kind these are no one is ignorant.[3]

Editors of newspapers soon found that their scurrility and attacks upon well-known citizens brought retribution. The two early eighteenth-century cases, those of James Franklin in 1722 and John Peter Zenger in 1734, resulting in penalties and jail sen-

---

[3] Vol. II, p. 255.

tences, showed that official skins were sensitive, but the Zenger case brought about a changed attitude on the liberty of the press. This attitude, however, was largely forfeited by the excessive licentiousness of newspapers in the last decade of the century. Finally the Sedition Act was passed in 1798, providing fines and imprisonment for any person convicted of printing or uttering false, scandalous, or malicious statements against the Government of the United States or either house of Congress. Twenty-five persons were arrested, eleven cases came to trial, and ten persons were convicted.[4] Not all of these cases were for newspaper utterances, and less than a dozen concerned newspaper publishers. During 1799 and 1800 Abijah Adams of the Boston *Independent Chronicle,* David Frothingham of the New York *Argus,* James Thomson Callender of the Richmond *Examiner,* Charles Holt of the New London *Bee,* Anthony Haswell of the Bennington *Vermont Gazette,* and William Durell of the *Mount Pleasant Register* were convicted and served jail sentences.

But the antipathy against the Alien and Sedition Acts helped to bring the downfall of the Federalists in the campaign of 1800, and the Acts expired. Suits for libel were now brought against editors under common law, and there were literally hundreds of

---

[4] F. M. Anderson "Alien and Sedition Laws" in American Historical Association *Annual Report* for 1912, p. 120.

cases during the first decade of the century. Fewer jail sentences were given. In 1802-04, a period of many intemperate attacks in newspapers, there were apparently only four editors jailed: John S. Lillie of the Boston *Constitutional Telegraph,* Harry Croswell of the Hudson *Wasp,* William Carlton of the *Salem Register,* and Nathaniel Willis of the Portland *Eastern Argus.* The majority of penalties consisted of fines, ranging from a few dollars to as much as $8,000. The number of trials was legion. James Cheetham of the New York *American Citizen* was constantly in trouble. The Hudson *Bee* of June 14, 1803, notes the fact that the latest libel suit against Cheetham was his thirteenth. Over sixty libel suits against William Duane had accumulated by 1806. And it was not only the papers of the large cities which were subject to suit. The editors of small-town newspapers were equally liable, as irate readers discovered real or fancied insults in editorial remarks.[5]

Another unwelcome result to the unwary editor was the challenge to a duel. It was a newspaper paragraph that caused the challenge by Aaron Burr to Alexander Hamilton in 1804, ending in Hamilton's

[5] Milton W. Hamilton, in his *Country Printer,* in the chapter "A Free Press," gives many details regarding libel suits. Incidentally, his book, published in 1936, although it concerns only New York State, is a mine of information on the careers of editors, printing-presses, apprentices, advertising, distribution, and other details of newspaper publication before 1830.

death Mathew Carey was challenged by the Federalist leader, Eleazer Oswald, and in the duel which followed received a wound which took over a year to heal. William Coleman became engaged in two duels. Thomas H. Benton, later to become a distinguished United States senator, was involved in several duels during his early newspaper life. John Mowry, editor of the *Louisiana Gazette,* was killed in a duel in 1813 by Ferdinand Ameling, a German captain of the United States Army. Frederick S. Fell, of the *Savannah Republican,* fought a duel in 1817 with a Dr. Proctor, but they fortunately adjusted their difficulties before either was seriously injured. Joseph M. Street, upon receiving a challenge for a duel from William W. Cooke, stated in his *Western World* of November 8, 1806, that he had concluded to file such challenges regularly as they were received and print a list of them in his paper. Duels were common to the time of the Civil War, especially in the South and West. There is need of a modern, comprehensive book on American duels. Lorenzo Sabine's book,[6] written nearly a hundred years ago, is still the best factual authority, although it includes European duels, and the American examples are not one-fifth of the total number.

The greatest peril for the newspaper editor was that he was always subject to personal attack. Benja-

---

[6] *Notes on Duels and Duelling* (3rd ed., 1859).

min Franklin, in an article written for the Philadelphia *Federal Gazette* of September 12, 1789, says:

> My proposal then is, to leave the liberty of
> the Press untouched, to be exercised in its full
> extent, force and vigour, but to permit the
> *liberty of the Cudgel* to go with it, *pari passu.*
> Thus, my fellow citizens, if an impudent writer
> attacks your reputation, dearer to you perhaps
> than your life, you may go to him as openly
> and break his head.

Franklin's advice, whether or not seriously in-
tended, was frequently followed. Benjamin Franklin
Bache was assaulted twice. On April 5, 1797, a man
named Humphries, who was the son of the builder
of the frigate *United States,* hammered him severely
on the head in retaliation for some remarks made in
the newspaper. Again, on August 8, 1798, he was
involved by John Ward Fenno in a quarrel in which
both drew blood. William Duane, who followed
Bache as editor of the *Aurora,* was attacked in May
1799 by a band of men who entered the newspaper
office, dragged Duane out, and beat him brutally.
Callender was assaulted and beaten in January 1803
by an irate reader. Coleman was often engaged in
quarrels and once was beaten so severely by an antag-
onist that his health was permanently affected.[1] The
most serious outbreak in American newspaper history was the attack on the office of the *Federal Re-*

[1] Allan Nevins, *The Evening Post* (1922), p. 49.

publican in Baltimore. On June 22, 1812, a mob destroyed the printing-office. The paper was then set up in Georgetown after a suspension of five weeks. But when publication was again attempted at Baltimore, on July 27, 1812, a mob assailed the office, which was manned by a defensive party of thirty men led by two old Revolutionary soldiers, General Henry Lee and General James M. Lingan. The final result of the conflict was that Alexander C. Hanson, the editor, was wounded and left for dead, General Lee was made a cripple for life, and General Lingan expired at the hands of the mob.

Perilous indeed was the life of an outspoken editor in those infant days of the Republic. But as government became more stabilized and lasting peace was established, newspaper vilification subsided. The demon of party bitterness departed and gave place to a general outburst of national feeling. In fact, the eight years of the Monroe administration, from 1817 to 1825, became known as "the era of good feelings." As the century progressed, newspaper animosities occasionally came to the surface. But gradually a higher standard of journalism manifested itself and the political hatreds of a century and a half ago are now only facts of history.

Women Newspaper Publishers

❧❧

I N THE early periods of American life
it is surprising that so many women acted as publishers of newspapers It is the usual conception that
women in colonial times served only in the home,
occupied with endless household cares and bearing
children. Generally speaking, this was true. Marriage
was customary and lasting, and large families were
the rule. Yet when husbands died the requirement
of supporting children was pressing, at least in the
interval before the next marriage. There was no law
or public opinion against women taking employ-
ment. Therefore women served frequently as tavern-
keepers, merchants, dressmakers, shop-keepers and
even as brewers, coach-makers and horse-shoers Generally necessity compelled.

The publisher of a newspaper was invariably an
important person in the community. A certain
amount of education was required, even if it was
self-education, and with so few schools a woman stood
as good a chance of being educated as her husband.
During the century of journalism before 1820 there
were thirty-two women who acted as publishers of
newspapers. Since no record in this respect has pre-

viously been compiled, the list of such women, with
the titles and dates of their papers, follows:

Mrs. Elizabeth Timothy, *South Carolina Gazette,* Charleston, 1739-46

Mrs. Cornelia Bradford, *American Weekly
Mercury,* Philadelphia, 1742-46

Mrs. Catherine Zenger, *New York Weekly
Journal,* New York, 1746-48

Mrs. Ann Franklin, *Newport Mercury,* Newport, 1762-63

Mrs. Sarah Goddard, *Providence Gazette,* Providence, 1765-68

Mrs. Anne Catharine Green, *Maryland Gazette,* Annapolis, 1767-75

Mrs. Clementina Rind, *Virginia Gazette,* Williamsburg, 1773-74

Mrs. Margaret Draper, *News-Letter,* Boston,
1774-75

Mary K. Goddard, *Maryland Journal,* Baltimore, 1775-84

Mrs. Mary Crouch, *Charleston Gazette,* Charleston, 1778-80

Mrs. Mary Crouch, *Salem Gazette,* Salem, 1781

Mrs. Hannah Watson, *Connecticut Courant,*
Hartford, 1778-79

Mrs. Elizabeth Boden, *South Carolina Weekly
Advertiser,* Charleston, 1783

Mrs. Ann Timothy, *Gazette of South Carolina,*
Charleston, 1783-85

Mrs. Ann Timothy, *State Gazette of South
Carolina,* Charleston, 1785-92

Mrs. Elizabeth Holt, *Independent Gazette,*
New York, 1784

Mrs. Elizabeth Holt, *New York Journal,* New
York, 1784-85

Mrs. Phebe Herbert, *Washington Spy*, Elizabethtown, Md., 1795-97

Mrs. Elizabeth Oswald, *Independent Gazetteer*, Philadelphia, 1795-96

Mrs. Margaret H. Bache, *Aurora*, Philadelphia, 1798

Mrs. Ann Greenleaf, *Argus*, New York, 1798-1800

Mrs. Ann Greenleaf, *Greenleaf's New York Journal*, New York, 1798-1800

Mrs. Ann Barber, *Newport Mercury*, Newport, 1800-09

Mrs. Sarah Hillhouse, *Monitor*, Washington, Ga., 1803-11

Mrs. Margaret Harrisson, *New York Weekly Museum*, New York, 1804-08

Mrs. Elizabeth Carlton, *Salem Register*, Salem, 1805

Mrs. Samuel Morse, *Georgia Republican*, Savannah, 1805

Mrs. Catherine Bose Dobbin, *American*, Baltimore, 1811-20

Mrs. Rebecca Bradford, *Nashville Examiner*, Nashville, 1814

Mrs. Charles C. Adams, *Republican Herald*, Poughkeepsie, 1814

Mrs. Patty Fessenden, *Reporter*, Brattleboro, 1815

Mrs. Jane Graham, *Greensburgh & Indiana Register*, Greensburgh, Pa., 1815-16

Mrs. Deborah W. Pleasants, *Virginia Argus*, Richmond, 1815

Mrs. Priscilla Harper, *Adams Centinel*, Gettysburg, 1816-19

Augustina Parsons, *Alabama Watchman*, Cahawba, 1820

Mrs. Susan Douglas, *Eastern Argus*, Portland, 1820.

The first woman publisher, as will be seen from the above list, was Elizabeth Timothy, 1730 Yet many years previous, in 1696, Dinah Nutheah the widow of William Nuthead, had been given leave to operate her husband's printing-press at Annapolis, in Maryland, and to print blank forms. The evidence regarding her brief career is convincingly given in Lawrence Wroth's *History of Printing in Colonial Maryland.* Even if she was so uneducated that she could not sign her name and despite the fact that no imprints of her press have survived, she can be honored as America's first woman printer. But it was Elizabeth Timothy, of Charleston, South Carolina, who was the earliest publisher of a newspaper. Immediately after the death of her husband, Lewis Timothy, publisher of the *South Carolina Gazette,* in December 1738, she announced that she would continue the paper as usual, describing herself as a poor afflicted widow with six small children and another hourly expected. Her husband had had a partnership agreement with Benjamin Franklin, who continued the agreement with the widow. He remarks in his *Autobiography:*

> . . . the business was continued by his widow, who, being born and bred in Holland, where, as I have been inform'd, the knowledge of accounts makes a part of female education, she not only sent me as clear a state as she could find of the transactions past, but continued to

account with the greatest regularity and exact-
ness every quarter afterwards, and managed
the business with such success, that she not
only brought up reputably a family of children, but, at the expiration of the term, was
able to purchase of me the printing-house, and
established her son in it.

As Franklin states, in this typically long sentence
of 103 words, Elizabeth Timothy owned and published the paper, but allowed the name of her son,
Peter Timothy, to appear in the imprint, and this
arrangement so continued until January 1, 1746.

The next woman publisher was Cornelia Bradford. Her husband, Andrew Bradford, had been
publishing at Philadelphia the *American Weekly
Mercury* since December 22, 1719, the third newspaper in the colonies, missing the honor of being
second to the *Boston Gazette* by only one day.
Andrew died November 24, 1742, and the widow
immediately began to issue the paper alone, using
mourning lines for the following six issues. After
three months she took Isaiah Warner into partnership, but at the end of a year and a half she assumed
sole proprietorship again and remained in control
until 1746, the year of the last known issue. Horatio
Gates Jones, in his *Address* on Andrew Bradford,
says of Cornelia Bradford: "She was remarkable for
beauty and talents, but not so much for the amenities
which give to female charms their crowning grace."

This seems to be in keeping with the Bradford family tradition that she broke up the partnership between her husband and her nephew, William Bradford, because of her opposition to the nephew's marriage.

The third woman journalist was Catherine Zenger, wife of John Peter Zenger, famous for his libel suit and the political activities of his paper, the *New York Weekly Journal*. He died in July 1746, and the widow took over the paper, publishing it for two years, when she turned it over to her stepson, John Zenger. She also printed pamphlets and almanacs in which her imprint was invariably "the Widow Catherine Zenger."

The next two newspaper women were of Rhode Island. Ann Franklin, who was wife of James Franklin and hence sister-in-law of Benjamin Franklin, came to Newport with her husband in 1727. James established a printing-press in that year, and his wife was a practical assistant. Upon his death in 1735 she continued the press, publishing many books and pamphlets, and thus becoming the first woman printer of New England. In 1748 she turned the establishment over to her son James, and it was he who commenced the *Newport Mercury* in 1758. In 1762 he died and the mother again assumed the burden as printer, conducting the newspaper until her death in April 1763. It is seldom that we can find comments on the early women printers, but in the case of Ann Franklin, Isaiah Thomas[1] supplies this interesting information:

> She was aided in her printing by her two daughters, and afterward by her son when he attained to a competent age. Her daughters were correct and quick compositors at case; and were instructed by their father whom they assisted. A gentleman who was acquainted with Ann Franklin and her family, informed me that he had often seen her daughters at work in the printing house, and that they were sensible and amiable women.

The other Rhode Island journalist was Sarah Goddard. Born an Updike and married to Dr. Giles Goddard of New London, she was the mother of William Goddard, famous throughout the colonies both in journalism and in political affairs. The son established the *Providence Gazette* in 1762. But three years later the paper was suspended for want of support, and William Goddard removed from Providence, leaving the press in charge of his mother. In August 1766 she revived the paper, printed by "Sarah Goddard and Company." With different partners she continued to publish it until November 1768, when she retired in favor of John Carter, and died in January 1770. Thomas describes her as a woman of excellent education and much ability.

Following down the list of women publishers, we next come to two Southern names. Anne Catharine

---

[1] *History of Printing* (1874 ed.), I, 195.

Green, born in Holland and brought to America when a child, married Jonas Green, printer. Jonas reëstablished the *Maryland Gazette* at Annapolis in 1745 and conducted it with much credit until his death in April 1767. The widow immediately assumed charge of the paper, asking thus for public support: "I Presume to address You for your Countenance to Myself and numerous Family, left, without your Favour, almost destitute of Support by the Decease of my Husband." Aided later by her two sons she continued the paper until her death, March 23, 1775, serving as public printer, issuing many volumes and pamphlets, and maintaining a high standard of typography.

The other Southern journalist was Clementina Rind, whose husband, William Rind, published the *Virginia Gazette* at Williamsburg. Upon his death in August 1773, she continued the paper for one year, until her own death in September 1774.

To list in detail the careers of all the other twenty-five women publishers would take more space than this address allows. The long list printed on a previous page shows that these women were well scattered throughout the colonies. Suffice it to say that in every case but one they were the widows of newspaper proprietors and assumed the burden left by their husbands, to obtain support for themselves and their families. The one exception was Augustina

Parsons, who herself established the *Alabama Watch-man* at Cahawba in 1820. She followed no previous publisher, and there was no other printer named Parsons during that period. She published the paper over the imprint of A. Parsons, and not until I found in a Savannah paper an advertisement of her proposal of publication did I even know her first name. She must have been a woman of rare courage and determination even if there is no evidence to show that her paper was continued for more than a few months. I have tried in vain to find more about Augustina Parsons. Cahawba was in Dallas County, Alabama, but the Dallas County Census for 1820 lists only one family of the name, Brooks Parsons, with three males in his family. It has to be assumed that Augustina, because of the name, was a woman.

Marriage and Death Records

✦✦✦✦✦✦✦✦✦✦✦✦✦✦✦✦✦✦✦✦✦✦✦✦✦✦✦✦✦✦✦✦✦✦✦

MARRIAGE AND death records in early newspapers are of the greatest value in the study of biography and genealogy. They generally gave little more than the bare facts—in marriages the names and residences of the contracting parties with the name of the minister, and in deaths only the name and residence with the age. Births were never noted.

Although the printers gave this service freely, it was often a source of income. To prevent being flooded with encomiums on the dead, they had at least some system of payment. This custom is well shown in the agreement which three leading Boston publishers adopted, as printed in the *Columbian Centinel* of October 3, 1798:

> For all Marriages, with a compliment to both or either of the parties, 25 Cents must be paid in advance. For all Deaths, with invitations to funerals, 25 cents will be expected in advance. All Characters of deceased persons, except eminent public characters, must be paid for as advertisements.

Otherwise there was no charge for notices, and there is no question but that this department of the newspaper was widely read. Often it was featured.

The Kennebunk *Eagle of Maine* grouped such notices under the headings of "Temple of Hymen" and "Temple of Mortality."

Occasionally a marriage notice caused the poetic wells to open, especially if there were punning possibilities in the names. The writing of poetry was a prevalent failing in the early days, and puns were accepted in the most learned circles. The *Salem Gazette* was a frequent offender in this respect. In its issue of September 25, 1810, the marriage at Boston of Mr. Jonathan Wild to Miss Harriet Joy was recorded, with the following poem:

> *First courtship, Wild with Joy ecstatic,*
> *The brighten'd hours of life beguil'd,*
> *Their marriage snatch'd the Joy emphatic,*
> *And left the parties doubly Wild.*

Again on November 9, 1810, following the notice of the marriage of Dr. Bates to Miss Eliza Hall, was this poem:

> *Now Hymen, turn'd fisher, had furnished his*
> *   stall;*
> *His baits being good, he has got a fine haul.*

Among other similar bursts of poetic wit I noticed this verse, in the Brooklyn *Long Island Star* of April 7, 1813, explaining the marriage of Mr. John Spader of Brooklyn to Miss Phebe Lott of Jamaica:

> *No* Spader *ever till'd the verdant plot,*
> *But found reward in some fair fruitful* Lott.

But the value of marriage and death records is far greater for biographical reference than it is for their inclusion in an anthology of poetry. Every newspaper printed the record of its local marriages and deaths, although such records before 1790 were confined to leading and prominent citizens. After the establishment of the United States and the spread of both newspapers and populations, the records became somewhat more comprehensive. Some newspapers made a surprisingly important feature of the marriage and death column The *Columbian Centinel* of Boston led in this regard. From about 1798 until the paper stopped in 1840, the publishers apparently copied every marriage and death record noted in the papers from all over the country which were received in exchange. As a result, each semi-weekly issue sometimes listed as many as fifty death notices, primarily of Massachusetts, secondarily of New England, and finally important names from distant states. The American Antiquarian Society, realizing the biographical value of this voluminous record, started ten years ago, with WPA help, to index all the marriages and deaths from 1784 to 1840. The marriages were listed and typed about five years ago in eight thick quarto volumes, containing about 120,000 names, or the record of 60,000 marriages. The death records, with 110,000 deaths, are now being typed and will constitute an even larger work. Unfortunately only six copies of these two sets were typed, with copies in the American Antiquarian Society, Library of Congress, New York Public Library, New England Historic Genealogical Society, and two other libraries. In both the marriages and the deaths there is only one alphabet for each series.

Another comprehensive undertaking is the listing of the marriages and deaths in the *New York Evening Post* from 1801 to 1887, compiled by Gertrude A. Barber for sale to several libraries. Unfortunately the work was issued in sections of only two or three years each, and there is an index only of last names. In Connecticut the record authorities, largely with WPA help, compiled indexes of the Connecticut marriages and deaths in important Connecticut newspapers, an exceedingly valuable series, but available only at Hartford. Several more limited listings have been undertaken elsewhere, chiefly for the early period. Most of these, however, were for local records only. The aid of all these lists in furnishing biographical data is incalculable.

Carriers' Addresses

❖❖

A FASCINATING phase in the history of newspapers is the Carrier's Address or the New Year's Verses. Distributed at doorways by the newsboy, these broadsides or leaflets brought in many a tip to eke out the boy's meager wage. They were never included in the serial numbering of the newspaper, such as an Extra, but were printed as a form of gratuity to the newsboy As a result, few people saved them, and they are so scarce today that the few found are generally the only known copies. The poetry ranges from the veriest doggerel to examples of superior verse, but they do preserve the common opinion on national and local politics, and they often give an insight into the social life of the community.

The earliest known examples are three written by Aquila Rose for the *American Weekly Mercury* in 1720, 1721, and 1722. No original broadsides can be found, but the three poems are reprinted in Rose's *Poems on Several Occasions*, Philadelphia, 1740. They are headed by the statement: "The three following Pieces, were wrote, by him, for the Boys who carried out the Weekly News-Papers to their Master's Customers, in Philadelphia; to whom, com-

monly, every New-Year's Day, they present Verses of
this Kind." The first is entitled "Wrote in 1720"
and begins:

> Full fifty Times have roul'd their Changes on,
> And all the Year's Transactions now are done;
> Full fifty Times I've trod, with eager Haste,
> To bring you weekly news of all Things past.
> Some grateful Thing is due for such a Task,
> Tho' Modesty itself forbids to ask;
> A Silver Thought, express'd in ill-shap'd Ore,
> Is all I wish; nor would I ask for more.

The poem goes on to state how news is brought by
ships and posts, and says:

> C———n may write, but B———————d's Art alone
> Distributes News to all th' expecting Town.

This refers to John Copson and Andrew Bradford,
the publishers of the *Mercury*. In the heading of the
poem, the use of the word "commonly," referring to
the distribution of such verses, presumably refers
to Aquila Rose's opinion expressed in 1740. At least
no American carrier's address is known before 1720,
and the only preceding American newspaper, the
Boston News-Letter, printed no verses that are mentioned. Nor can any broadside carrier's verses be
found for English newspapers before 1720. Occasional English broadside poems are found for other
types of services rendered, such as bellmen, lamp-
lighters, or bakers' lads, even as early as 1686. The
Huth collection, for instance, had several broadsides
of this character, of the early eighteenth century.

In the *Mercury* verses for 1721 and 1722 the author summarizes events in Europe, with brief reference to America, but especially to his native city:

> *Or, Philadelphia's Pile with Pleasure trace,*
> *And paint the Beauties of this Rising Place,*
> *How regular the Plan! How bright the View!*
> *Her Neighbour's Wonder, and their Envy too.*

The earliest broadside carrier's address that I have been able to locate is that issued for the *American Weekly Mercury* on January 1, 1735. Although undated, it is bound in the American Antiquarian Society's practically complete file just preceding the issue of January 7, 1735. It has a large cut of Mercury at the top and begins:

> *There's not an Ear that is not deaf*
> *But listens to the News;*
> *There's not a Tongue that is not stiff*
> *That will the Tale refuse.*

After this sprightly beginning, the poem summarizes the news of the world and ends:

> *If these vast Things, kind Sirs, content,*
> *Of such you shall have many;*
> *But, if you think my Time misspent,*
> *Then give me ne'er a Penny.*

The next broadside verses discovered are those issued by Benjamin Franklin for the *Pennsylvania Gazette,* later to be described.

Judging from the examples which have been preserved, I would not believe that the custom of printing New Year's verses was general in the smaller towns throughout the eighteenth century. After 1800, with the beginning of violent party politics, the verses more frequently appeared until gradually it seemed as if almost every paper in the country issued its carrier's address. But about 1870 the custom began to fall off, probably because it was beginning to become commercial and the larger influential newspapers considered it undignified. Frederic Hudson, writing in 1873,[1] says:

> The newspaper Carriers' Address is probably the last of its class. Thirty or forty years ago, the Lamplighters, the Watchmen, and others employed by the authorities of Boston, annually issued addresses in rhyme, but without reason, and received considerable sums of money. The *New York Herald* was the first to put a stop to those of the Carriers in New York. The *Journal of Commerce* followed. The *Philadelphia Ledger,* instead of an address in rhyme, got out, in 1870, a very useful and valuable Almanac, which Mr. Childs, its proprietor, sent to each subscriber free.

In commenting upon Mr. Hudson's statement, I notice that in the Antiquarian Society's broadsides there are several examples of New Year addresses issued by the watchmen and the scavengers at Boston in the earlier nineteenth century.

In the 1880's, commercialism was prevalent, and New Year's verses were printed without the name of a distinguishing paper and sold to any carriers who

---

[1] *Journalism in the United States* (1873), p. 99.

would buy. One of these examples in 1886 was so all-embracing that it was entitled "New Year's Address to the Patrons of Sunday and Daily Papers." Finally the custom degenerated merely to the distribution of Christmas or New Year's cards. The last genuine carrier's address I have seen was dated in the year 1904.

During this long period of more than a century of poetical publication, there were many outstanding carriers' addresses. *The New York Weekly Museum* address for 1790 is headed by a woodcut of a boy delivering a paper at a doorway, one of the few examples of illustration. The quality of the poetry began to improve in the 1790's as poets became less influenced by the literary yoke of the parent country. The *Boston Advocate* in 1833 abandoned the broadside poem for a rhyming pamphlet of eight pages. The Salem newspapers in the 1830's occasionally issued pamphlets in prose, instead of rhyme. The size began to increase. The *Albany Journal* in 1839 printed a quarto four-page pamphlet with nearly one hundred verses. The New York papers generally printed large broadsides, and *Brother Jonathan's* address for 1840, as would be expected, was an elephant folio.

The subject matter, especially in the stormy period previous to the Civil War, ran heavily to political discussion. Some, however, refrained from politics, such as the *Spirit of the Times* which in 1839 produced an elaborate address chronicling the names of scores of theatre favorites, sportsmen, and race horses. The Virginia *Lexington Gazette* for 1840 presented as half of the broadside a wall calendar for 1841, one of the earliest examples of its kind. The *Essex Register* for 1841, the *New York Tribune* for 1844, and the *New York Express* for 1850 produced large broadsides with elaborate borders of printer's ornaments—more, I believe, than I have ever seen on a single sheet. Striving for typographical superiority was common.

The poetry, as noted above, was highly varied. Before the addresses became essentially political, the versifier generally accented the hardships endured by the newsboy The *Boston Evening Post* verses for 1767 begin:

> *Oft, gen'rous Patron, to regale your Taste,*
> *The Summer's Suns, and Winter Storms I've fac'd.*
> *How many Annual Miles fatigu'd I've trod,*
> *Thro' Depths of Snow, and Magazines of Mud!*
> *Now at your Door I once again appear,*
> *To wish all Blessings crown your Happy Year.*

A Portland paper of 1807 under the heading of "The Carrier's Hint" says:

> *No pelting of the pit'less storm*
> *The tempest in its various form,*
> *Nor frost, nor rain, nor drifting snow,*
> *Forbids the Carrier to go.*

The Boston *Idiot* poem for 1819 concludes:

> *I've toiled for you thro' storms of hail and rain,*
> *Hard was my lot, though very small my gain.*
> *Now if you'll but unfold your purse and heart*
> *And grant a FEE—I'll thankfully depart.*

During the four years of the Civil War the poems were martial and patriotic, but opposite in opinion, depending on which side of Mason and Dixon's Line they were published. The *Richmond Enquirer* on December 25, 1861, had a long poem of which the following is a sample verse:

> *Since last your carrier sang his annual lay,*
> *Eclipse hath fallen on a nation's day!*
> *Sad, in its grave, the dead old Union sleeps,*
> *And on its tomb no Angel vigil keeps.*

The Buffalo *Commercial Advertiser* for 1862 thus apostrophizes the times:

> *Amid the clang of arms, the clash of arms,*
> *   The cannon's roar, the startling trumpet's din,*
> *Amid alarms, War's fierce and wild alarms,*
> *   The fresh young Year came in.*

The amount of *pourboire* expected by the carrier was generally left to the customer. Many of the verses conclude with such a sentiment as "Remember the poor printer's Devil" or "Be bounteous to the Printer's Boy." Sometimes the sentiment is more definite, such as "I won't refuse a six pence" and "Please keep the cents and—give the silver." The boy who carried the *Massachusetts Magazine* in 1794 asked for "a Shilling, Six pence, or a Cent," and the lad who distributed Dunlap's *American Daily Advertiser* in 1795 suggested progressively a cent, a five-penny-bit, a 'leven-penny piece, or a quarter. But the most hopeful request was in the *Boston Gazette* for 1805:

> *You hav'nt sir,—I cannot doubt you—*
> *A pistareen or so about you;*
> *Not that I want the small donation,*
> *I only ask'd for information.*

Joseph T. Buckingham, in his *Personal Memoirs,*[2] records that when he distributed the New Year's Address of the *Greenfield Gazette,* on January 1, 1797, he amassed the unheard-of wealth of $6.75.

Almost invariably the carrier's address was not signed. A friend of the printer, or often the publisher himself, generally contributed the verse. The writing of poetry was habitual in the eighteenth century, and both young and old indulged in it. The absence of the pleasures which are brought to homes in modern times made many turn to self-expression in poetry for diversion. Occasionally an insignificant poet, or even the carrier himself, signed the verses. For instance Job Weeden, Salem newsboy, presented the address to the customers of the *Essex Gazette* in 1772. The *Providence Gazette* verses of 1797 are signed by William Gerrish. David Jones, the carrier, admits to writing the poems for the *Christian Disciple* for 1815 and 1817. A Newport address for 1837 was signed by

---

[2] 1852, Vol. 1, p. 27.

John Barlow. The Virginia *Lexington Gazette* address of 1840 is signed "W. Downs, Carrier." In frequent cases a friend, or a literary annalist, has penciled the name of the writer at the end of the poem. The address of the Philadelphia *Aurora* for 1830 thus has the annotation "by Charles West Thomson." The exceptionally amusing prose address to the patrons of the *Salem Gazette,* an eight-page pamphlet entitled "Rip Van Winkle in Salem," has the notation that it was written by Fitch Pool of Danvers. The Harrisburg *Telegraph* poem of 1866 says "By Dr. Egle." Buckingham, in his *Personal Memoirs,* quoted above, says that the *Greenfield Gazette* address of 1797 was written by Samuel Elliot, then a clerk in a store at Guilford, Vermont. Buckingham also records that as the youngest apprentice it was his duty to distribute the New Year's Address. This lowliest employe in the printing office was generally called the "Printer's Devil," a name of much antiquity in the history of typography.

These anonymous poems were often written by poets who were well known or were later to acquire fame. Since their efforts were veiled under anonymity, it is only through contemporary letters or journals, or through casual remarks by fellow scribes, that their names are now known. Sometimes such authors were sufficiently proud of their efforts to include the verses in published collected poems.

THE YEARLY VERSES

Of the Printer's Lad, who carrieth about the *Pennsylvania* GAZETTE, to the Customers thereof.

Jan. 1. 1739.

The spreading of NEWS.

BEGIN, mercurial Muse, with quickest Ears,
With quickest Tongues, with quickest Hopes & Fears:
First *name* the *stripling Tatlers*, who between
Their Sports on Pavements, & those on the Green,
Pick up a Thousand Tidings by the way;
If true or false, all's Fish, and all their Prey.
Next them, and scarce a single Step behind
Are *Betty*, *Molly*, *Susy*, unconfin'd;
All of the Errand-Class, the Toilet, Tea,
The *Needle-Artists*, and each wandering She:
Lively they hear, they see, supply, relate;
Talk the short Day out, and in sleeping prate.
'Twas ever thus with either Sex in Youth,
NEWS they regarded, but unheeded Truth.
Mercurial call'd, for sprightly Chat and Sense,
From *Mercury*, the God of Eloquence.

News from without-Doors, oft' spreads hurrying in.
And simple Stuff too soon improves to Sin:
The Tale new-form'd, and strengthen'd takes its Flight,
Sent forth for Laughter, Slander, or to fright;
Dress'd up by elder Tongues, the *Nurse*, the *Prude*,

Aquila Rose's three poems written for Bradford's *American Weekly Mercury* in 1720, 1721, and 1722 have previously been mentioned. Benjamin Franklin followed the custom of "Yearly Verses" for many years, although the first surviving example is that for 1739. Of the pre-Revolutionary *Pennsylvania Gazette* addresses the American Antiquarian Society has those for 1739, 1740, 1741, 1743, 1748, 1749, 1752, and 1772. It is reasonable to believe that Franklin himself wrote these verses in the early period. He was addicted to writing poetry, evidenced chiefly by his rhymes in Poor Richard. Some of the lines are reminiscent of his style and thought. In "The Yearly Verses of the Printer's Lad," January 1, 1739, the poem is headed "The Spreading of News." In referring to the "Stripling Tatlers" who believed all that they heard, the poem reads:

> *'Twas ever thus with either Sex in Youth,*
> News *they regarded, but unheeded Truth.*

The poem ends by contrasting the rumors and romances of gossip with the accuracy of the news in the *Gazette*. The 1740 Verses draw a moral between those who lock their doors and those who leave their households unguarded and consequently have their treasures stolen. One couplet reads:

> *An honest Industry becomes a Man,*
> *And to preserve his Freedom if he can.*

The Yearly Verses for 1743 describe strife throughout the world, with the conclusion:

> *How happy Pennsylvania's Plains*
> *Where only civil Discord reigns.*

Perhaps if these early verses were reprinted, some
able students of Franklin would find analogies or
similarities to show that he was the author.

Joel Barlow, who was one of the most prolific of
of our early poets and seldom missed the opportunity
of dashing off a rhyme, wrote several anonymous
New Year's Verses. Theodore A. Zunder, in his
Early Days of Joel Barlow,[3] records that Barlow wrote
"The Post-Boy's Present to his Customers" for a New
Haven newspaper in 1779, the carrier's address for
the *American Mercury* in 1785 and 1786, and the
New Year's poems for the *Connecticut Courant* in
1787. Printed copies of these, in the form of broadsides, are in the Barlow Papers in the Harvard College Library. Also Joel Munsell, in an annotated note
in the American Antiquarian Society's copy of the
Typographical Miscellany, states that Sidney Babcock told him in 1869 that Barlow wrote the carrier's
address for Babcock & Haswell's Springfield *Massachusetts Gazette* in 1783. Barlow's friend Elisha Babcock was later to become his partner in publishing
the *American Mercury* in 1784 and 1785.

---

[3] 1934, pp. 64, 176, 189, 200,

Philip Freneau, as noted in Wegelin's *Early American Poetry*, composed several New Year's Verses: one for Francis Wrigley, the carrier, in 1783, verses for both the *Pennsylvania Evening Post* and the *Freeman's Journal* in 1783, verses for the *Pennsylvania Gazette*, the *Freeman's Journal*, and a Charleston paper in 1784, one for the *Freeman's Journal* in 1785, and one for an unknown paper in 1786. Four of these were reprinted in the 1786 and 1795 editions of his *Poems*, and some are known by original printed broadsides.

Richard Alsop, the Connecticut poet, wrote the carrier's address for the Hartford *American Mercury* in 1793, an interesting poem with scores of allusions to New England characters and wants.[4] I have not located the broadside poem, but it is printed in the newspaper of January 7, 1793.

Selleck Osborn wrote the New Year's Address for the Danbury *Republican Farmer* in 1805,[5] for the Hartford *American Mercury* in 1811, for the Wilmington *American Watchman* in 1817, and for unnamed papers in 1820 and 1821. The last four poems were reprinted in his *Poems*, published in 1823.

William Biglow, well known for his humorous poetry in the early part of the century, wrote a lengthy and entertaining New Year's Address for the

---

[4] K. P. Harrington, *Richard Alsop* (1939), p. 60.
[5] Reprinted in Sag Harbor *Suffolk Gazette* of Feb. 4, 1805.

New England Galaxy in 1826, in which he paid his respects to all the newspapers and editors of Boston.

John Greenleaf Whittier, as evidenced by Currier's authoritative Bibliography,[6] wrote several New Year's addresses. those for the Haverhill *Essex Gazette* for 1828 and 1829, the *New England Weekly Review* for 1831, and the *Pennsylvania Freeman* for 1839. Most of these are preserved as printed broadsides.

John Neal wrote the "Address for the New Year" for the Boston *Yankee* in 1829. Neal was editor of the *Yankee* and an accomplished novelist and poet.

Nathaniel Hawthorne's two contributions in this field are exceptionally scarce and desirable. In 1838 he wrote "Time's Portraiture" as the carrier's address for the *Salem Gazette*. This broadside was again printed by the *Salem Gazette* on New Year's in 1853. In 1839 he wrote "The Sister Years" also for the *Salem Gazette*. It was a pamphlet of eight pages, and was reprinted by the *Salem Gazette* as its carrier's address in 1892.

Daniel Webster wrote the carrier's address for the *Dartmouth Gazette* of Hanover in 1803, which is so noted in the Dartmouth College copy of the newspaper, although it does not possess the original broadside. Further research will reveal the names of many more famous authors who could not resist the tempta-

---

[6] *Bibliography of John Greenleaf Whittier* (1937), pp. 12, 42, 179, 308, 309.

tion to invoke the muse, to befriend the publisher, and to help the newsboy, even if they did choose to remain anonymous.

Apparently the largest collections of carriers' addresses are in the Brown University Library and the American Antiquarian Society, each of which owns nearly six hundred broadsides. The Historical Society of Pennsylvania owns a remarkable collection of over eighty broadside verses, all issued for Boston newspapers in the eighteenth century beginning with 1761. Gerald D. McDonald of the New York Public Library has long been making a bibliography of carriers' addresses and already has 2,756 in his checklist. When he finds the opportunity to examine further collections, it is to be hoped that he will issue the results of his study in printed form.

William Goddard's Additions to Thomas'
History of Printing

❖◆❖◆❖◆❖◆❖◆❖◆❖◆❖◆❖◆❖◆❖◆❖◆❖◆❖◆❖◆❖◆❖◆❖◆❖◆❖

WILLIAM GODDARD, one of the most famous of eighteenth-century printers, was a long-time friend of Isaiah Thomas. Slightly older, he was born in 1740 and died in 1817. His printing career covered newspapers and general printing at Providence, Philadelphia, and Baltimore. Thomas in his *History* gives much space to Goddard, whom he regarded as capable and talented. Goddard was an ardent Whig, and because of his activities in establishing the colonial postoffice was appointed surveyor of postroads by Franklin. Goddard had expected the position of comptroller of the postoffice, which office, however, Franklin gave to his son-in-law, Richard Bache. He never forgave Franklin for this and subsequent slights, and in a letter to Thomas, written in 1811, attacked the memory of Franklin unmercifully. At the same time he wrote Thomas two letters with corrections and additions to the *History of Printing,* in which work he was much interested. In fact, no printer, with the exception of Thomas, knew more about political affairs of the Revolutionary period than Goddard. Although these two letters do not contain too much of value for the history of printing, they do include a few facts, and since they have never been printed, they are made a part of the present paper. The most important contributions are those concerning his own career, especially in the establishing of the *Constitutional Courant* at Woodbridge in 1765. There are a few facts also regarding printing at Barbados, Antigua, and Jamaica. He was incorrect, of course, in calling Ellis Huske, the early Boston publisher, "Estis." The two letters are in Volume 6 of the Isaiah Thomas Papers, in the American Antiquarian Society. The letter regarding Franklin is not printed.

History of Printing

King Geo. II, of England, not only entertained a great regard for the art of Printing, but his Queen, Caroline, considered it of the utmost Importance to Mankind. Under the Impression that a Printing-Office would prove an excellent School for her Son, the Great Duke of Cumberland, she caused one to be established, for his Benefit, at Windsor Castle, where, under the Instruction of a capable Man, the Royal Duke (then a Youth) was taught the "Art and Mystery," which proved highly useful in his future Progress thro' Life, by giving him Habits of accuracy in literary Composition. The Duke always venerated eminent Men of the Profession and, amongst many whom he honoured with social Visits, he was particularly attentive to Dr. Franklin, with whom he frequently conversed, and played a Game of

Chess. The Printing Apparatus is said to be now at Windsor.

Vol. I, p. 150 *William Brown* and *Thomas Gilmore,* Partners, 1764.

329 *Ellis Huske,* postmaster.—Quere if *Ellis* should not be *Estis.*

410 Instead of *James Hunter,* it should be *William Hunter.*

427 After the words a Printing Press at Providence, it might be added—where, by appointment of Dr. Franklin (recommended by James Parker, Esq: Sec. & Comptroller of the Gen. P.O.) he became D. Postmaster.

428 By advice, and under the Patronage of his Friend Parker, he left his Printing house, Post-Office, &c. in the Care of his mother.

430 Removed to Philad. from motives of maternal affection.

Vol. II, p. 58 For *James Crukshank,* read *Joseph.*

107 4th line for *Robert Hunter* read *William Hunter.*

121 Here in *1752* is wrong. It must have been after the Discontinuance of the Magazine, which continued in 1759.

140 Mary K. Goddard was an expert & correct Compositor of Types.

180 Brown & Gilmor. The former a Scotchman. The latter a native of Philad'a.

212 *Ellis Huske.* Q'r if not *Estis.*

231 *Ellis* Huske—Quere if this name should not be *Estis Huske.*

232 *Ellis* Huske again—Q'r if not Estis.

322 Instead of *Constitutional Gazette*—it should be *Constitutional Courant,* in *three places.* It was printed at *Woodbridge,* and the Impression sent, by Express, to New York, where the Sale was rapid & extensive. The Government was alarmed at the patriotic Fervor it produced. It was sold by *Laurence* Sweeny.

353 Error respecting Lee—General Charles. *See Corrections in Book.*

354 Gen. Lee's Estate *was not confiscated*—the Profits withheld *pro Tem.* See Correction in margin of the History.

I think while I lived in Philad I used to exchange News-Papers with Mr. *John Anderson,* Printer at Barbados.

A well conducted Gazette was published at St. John's, Antigua by Mr. *John Mearns.* He continued it in 1779. He was a man of Talents & pleasantry. The following is a note to one of his Correspondents.

"The Printer's respectful Compliments wait on *Pacificus,* and hopes he will excuse him from the mortifying Task of publishing his own Blunders in repeated Erratums. The pressing Hour of Publication will not admit of a circumspect revisal of a News-Paper, nor did any Person, the least acquainted with the Nature of Printing (without disappointment) expect to see correctness in a periodical literary Publication. The Printer, however, as well to save himself Trouble as to oblige *Pacificus,* will give him and the World an Errata, by the lump, as follows:

"The multifarious Blunders & Errors of the Printer of this Gazette, and his Compositors, whether technical or typographical, his worthy Correspondents and judicious, candid, and endulgent Readers, are requested to overlook, or excuse and correct, from this Time (March 17th, 1779) forth, and forever more, *Amen.*"

2d Vol. p. 428 *John Checkley* was for some Time a regular Bookseller (as I have understood) at Boston, afterwards rec'd Episcopal Ordination in England, & was many years Rector of St. John's Church in this Town

[Providence], where he was held in high
Estimation for his Learning, Philan-
thropy, Wit, and many endearing Vir-
tues. Two of his Granddaughters are
living, in the State of New-York. There
are many curious & laughable anecdotes
related of this Gentleman, shewing the
Brilliancy of his Wit and the comic
Singularity of his Humour.

2d Vol.

Page 455 Note. Quere—if John A——n should not
be Andrew A——n.
So also in Towne's Recantation—same
page. Be pleased to examine.

504 For *Constitutional Gazette*, read *Constitutional Courant*. See also p. 322, the
same Error.
Quere if Keith, William, Governor of
Pennsylvania, was not Knight—Sir William &c.

p. 562 Last line—*Huske, Ellis*—Q'r if not *Estis*.
["No" in handwriting of I. Thomas.]

No Time to *copy* or *marshal* any part of
what I have here *paraded*. I write more for
your *amusement* then your *use*, sensible that
much of my *Crudities* will only serve to light a
Cigar occasionally.

William Goddard loaned a Press and Types
to Mr. George Richards, a Relative, and aided
in establishing a Printing House in Alex'a.
Virginia, where he published the Virg'a. Gazette, the *first Paper* that made its appearance
there. In G's exertions to serve & promote
Richards, he sunk £500. The Death of Richards precluded all Hopes of Indemnification.

W. G. contemplated the Establishm't of a
Press at Al [exandria] in the Beginning of 1770
—but the Death of his invaluable Parent, Sarah
Goddard, uniting with other misfortunes,
checked his promising Plan in the Bud.

W. G. also made preparation for opening a

Printing House in Norfolk—but his Plan was
defeated by untoward Events.

By way of Mem'a. I have hastily scrawled
over the few Particulars contained in this Sheet.
I am sensible they possess little, very little,
value. However, if they can be rendered, *in
any Degree,* acceptable, the *Scraps* are much
at your Service.

I have sent the hastily corrected Sheets of the
History of Printing directed to you at Worcester, to the Care of your Son, at Boston.

                              Prov. April 22, 1811
Isaiah Thomas, Esq. My best Wishes await
your Family & Mr. Sheldon.

The first Almanack, printed in Providence
was calculated by the ingenious Dr. Benj'n
West, for 1763—Wm Goddard, Printer.

Woodbridge, New Jersey, is a Township—
but not a borough town.

When Commodore Nicholson was President
of the Whig Club, he was then (in 1777) com-
mander of the United States frigate Virginia
(See p. 135, vol. II). The Virginia was captured
by the British in Chesapeake.

Page 449, vol. 2d. For *James Crukshank* read
Joseph Crukshank—opened, &c.

[Endorsed]:

> Isaiah Thomas Esq;
>   Worcester,
>   Massachusetts.

To the Care of Mr. Isaiah Thomas, jun. Bookseller in Boston. To be forwarded by a
private Hand.

During the Troubles occasioned by the Stamp Act of 1765, cautious & opulent Men in some parts of the Continent discont'd or altered the Titles of their Papers. I believe Wells suspended his—Hall & Sellers called their Gaz. *"Important Occurrences."*

After Defeat of Braddock, July 9, 1755, and the assemblage of an army at Lake St. Sacrament, now Lake George, where, Sept. 30, Sr. Wm. Johnson gained a victory over Baron Dieskeau & his Regulars & Savages (taking the Baron Prison'r Sir Wm. having only Provincials, under his Command) much Business was done at the New-Haven P. Office and many Posts established to the army &c. &c. under the Direction of Franklin, Parker, &c. At 15 I was sent with a Rider from New-Haven to Middletown & Hartford, thence to N. London, and round by Seaboard to N.H. to estimate the Expense. Great Changes have taken place since in this & every other Quarter of this great Continent. If I was now as *alert,* you would soon see me at Worcester.

In 1758, I went to N.York & Woodbridge to assist in the offices there—as I have already mentioned.

Mr. Burbank, to whom I committed my Letter to you of the 9th having given me a little more Time, I have improved it to furnish you with a few very loose, crude & incorrect Sketches. I doubt whether they will prove of any material Service to you—but they may *whet up* your Memory, & lead to Inqueries of Persons possessing more Information, Patience, Recollection & Arrangement.

When I went to New-York in 1758 the American Company of Commedians, under the management of David Douglas, Esq. a Gent. of honour & Talents (who married the Widow Hallam) performed in a Sail-Loft on Cruger's Dock! Douglas was afterwards King's Printer in Jamaica, a Master in Chancery, a Magistrate, &c. patronized by his Countryman Sir Basil Keith. Douglas made a Fortune. You have done the same—God bless his memory—and grant that you may *very long enjoy yours,* crowned with *every* Blessing.

I have written hastily to my worthy Friend Sheldon by Mr. Burbank. I put my Letter under Cover to you. Permit me to recommend your consulting him respecting your Work. He can greatly assist you, and may be relied on.

I know you are industrious & indefatigable, & I hope those you write to for Information, will most cheerfully & promptly give it.

The Marquis de Montcalm succeeded Baron de Deskeau, who was dreadfully wounded & went to Bath, Eng. Montcalm defeated Abercombie (Gen. James) who attempted to Storm the Lines, &c. of Ticonderoga, July 8, 1758—and his gallant Career was finished with Wolfe 's on The Plains of Abraham, Sept. 13, 1759, when they both fell, as you have read.

Excuse me for introducing articles foreign to your Design.

Robert Wells left Charleston previous to the American War, and lived independently in London. John cont'd the Paper (Gazette) with a large Book-Store in 1776. Tho' he fought bravely in Georgia in the American Cause, he offended beyond Forgiveness by uniting with the British (to save his Property) after the Surrender of Charleston. He wished to return from Nassau—but was not permitted.

[Endorsed]:

Isaiah Thomas, Esq.

Worcester,

Massachusetts.

Mr. Burbank

News Rooms

An INTERESTING custom in newspaper history was the establishment in the early 1800's of news rooms at nearly all of the larger towns. Somewhat akin to this idea was a project carried out at a much earlier day at Bridgeton, New Jersey. Here in December 1775, and continuing for two months, a weekly paper called "The Plain Dealer," consisting of essays but with topics relating to the problems of the colonies, was written out in manuscript and posted up in Matthew Potter's tavern. It enabled readers to gather at a central meeting place and peruse a weekly publication, which they would not trouble, or perhaps could not afford, to purchase.

Soon after 1800, reading rooms sprang up in several towns. In Boston the Anthology Reading Room was established in 1806, with 160 subscribers, and making available all the leading newspapers of the country, as well as a few foreign publications. In 1808 Samuel Gilbert established at Boston what may have been the first commercial news room in the country. It was located in the Exchange Coffee House, erected in 1808, with its "Reading Room and Marine Diary" on the entrance floor, where newspaper files could be

consulted. Samuel Topliff took over the reading
room in 1811, and soon made the establishment the
most famous in the country, noted for its accurate
marine news and for the usefulness of its service to
merchants and subscribers.[1]

In New York, John Howard Payne in 1811 opened
a reading room, where could be found the most important newspapers and magazines of the day. Eastburn, Kirk & Co. established a reading room in 1814,
later to be succeeded by J. Eastburn & Co.[2] Charleston had a news room in 1813, where the terms were
ten dollars for subscribers and strangers one dollar
a month.[3] In fact, almost every city and larger town
before 1820 had its news room, where leading newspapers were regularly filed. To enumerate them
would require a lengthy chapter and necessitate an
exacting study of early newspaper advertisements.
Unfortunately there is no record of a news room
proprietor preserving his files for posterity.

---

[1] See *Bostonian Society Publications,* VIII, 123; and *Topliff's Travels,*
edited by Ethel S. Bolton (1906).
[2] *New York Evening Post,* Feb. 15, 1811; *Concise Description of New
York* (1814), p. 39.
[3] *Charleston Courier,* Mar. 5, 1813.

Early Collections of Newspapers

PUBLISHERS OCCASIONALLY realized that newspapers would become sources for historical study, and acted in different ways to make their journals of value. In some instances they provided their papers with annual indexes. John Fenno, who published the *Gazette of the United States* at New York and Philadelphia, provided a title-page and index for the first three volumes, from 1789 to 1792. The Norwich, Connecticut, *Weekly Register* of 1791-95 printed at the end of each volume an excellent index, which included the record of marriages and deaths, and even indexed advertisements. The Suffield, Connecticut, *Impartial Herald* of 1797-99 also printed an index, but one of no particular usefulness and not even alphabetical. The *Balance,* published at Hudson and later at Albany, included Indexes, or rather Tables of Contents, for 1802-1808 and for 1811, in which years the paper was published in quarto form. The most useful indexes were prepared for *Niles' Weekly Register,* a magazine rather than a newspaper. This excellent publication provided indexes for each volume from the establishment in 1811 to 1849, and even issued a cumulative index for 1811-17.

Two newspaper proprietors sought to have their papers permanently preserved by presenting files to certain libraries. Noah Webster, in his New York *Spectator* of July 3, 1799, offered to present his paper to the New-York Society Library, the Philadelphia Library Company, the Massachusetts Historical Society, and the colleges of Columbia, Princeton, Yale, Rhode Island, Harvard, and Dartmouth, with the request that the papers should be bound and preserved. Apparently Yale, Dartmouth, and the Massachusetts Historical Society accepted the gift and its requirement and have the files today. Isaiah Thomas records in his accounts under date of September 26, 1818, the expense of $60 each for sending bound files of the *Massachusetts Spy* for "30 years past" to the Massachusetts Historical Society, the New-York Historical Society, the American Philosophical Society, and the American Academy of Arts and Sciences. The first three libraries still have the files, and the American Academy file went to the Boston Athenæum.

Isaiah Thomas was the most prominent collector of newspapers of his day. He inserted an advertisement in the Baltimore *Federal Republican* (and presumably other newspapers) from April 21 to May 13, 1809, that he would purchase or accept newspaper

files before 1775, and listed the titles of the newspapers which he especially desired. Incidentally, he
advertised that he also wanted to purchase the *Bay
Psalm Book* of 1640. Whether this advertisement re-
sulted favorably, or because of personal friendships
with early printers, it is a fact that some of Thomas'
most important files were acquired by him in 1810.
In that year he purchased the *American Weekly
Mercury,* 1719-46, for $70; the *Pennsylvania Gazette,*
1737-83, for $180; the *New York Gazette,* 1765-69,
for $30; and the *New York Journal,* 1767-68, for $10.
Previously, in 1808, he acquired from Ebenezer
Hazard of Philadelphia the *Pennsylvania Chronicle,*
1767-72, for $32, and the *Pennsylvania Evening Post,*
1775-82, for $24. Other files which he purchased, but
did not note the year, were the *Boston Evening Post,*
1735-75, for $60; Zenger's *New York Weekly Journal,*
1733-51, for $30; and *Rivington's Gazette,* 1773-83,
for $40. Some of these were the publisher's own files,
and several of them are today the most complete
known. His files of the *Boston News-Letter,* in fifteen
volumes, cost him $30, and of the *Boston Gazette,*
in ten volumes, $22.50, but these were incomplete
files and no date of acquisition is entered.

Next to Isaiah Thomas, the greatest collector of
newspapers was a German, Christoph Daniel Ebeling
of Hamburg. As part of his scheme of writing a history of America, which he partially completed in

seven volumes published from 1793 to 1816, he entered into correspondence with many American scholars in order to acquire materials. His most consistent correspondent was the Reverend William Bentley of Salem. Although Ebeling obtained newspapers from Jeremy Belknap, Mathew Carey, and others, by far the greatest part of his newspaper collection came from Bentley. Because of his connection with Salem newspapers, especially with the *Salem Register,* Bentley was able to save all the newspapers which came by way of exchange, and send them to Ebeling by the most convenient ship. In return Ebeling sent Bentley hundreds of volumes of German newspapers and periodicals. When Ebeling died in 1817 he had accumulated a remarkable collection of American newspapers, which he had bound in both a geographical and chronological arrangement. In 1818 Israel Thorndike purchased the entire Ebeling collection and presented it to Harvard University. As it stands now on the shelves it comprises 312 large bound volumes of newspapers, covering with few exceptions from the year 1795 to 1808. It is the best existing collection of American newspapers for those fourteen years and is worth at a low estimate $50,000. The German periodicals which Ebeling sent to Bentley, also covering from 1795 to 1808, came through Bentley's will to the American Antiquarian Society. Their market value might be $200. Twenty years ago they were exchanged with the Harvard College Library for some South American newspapers.

Other scholars in America collected and bound files of newspapers, but only with a local basis. Jefferson gathered a file of the *Virginia Gazette* extending from 1741 to 1783, which he had bound in thirteen volumes. Most of the pre-Revolutionary years' were unique. The entire file, with most of Jefferson's books, was destroyed in the Library of Congress fire of December 24, 1851. William Plumer, Governor of New Hampshire, collected and bound New Hampshire files, which are now in the Boston Athenæum. Samuel Parker, of Roxbury, bound certain Boston files, which are now in the Antiquarian Society. Many public characters, such as Washington, Adams, and others, received and read a considerable number of newspapers, but no evidence is afforded that these were bound. It remains for Isaiah Thomas to be the only American collector who foresaw the value of newspapers and gathered them for preservation.